W9-AOK-597

Gymnastics

Gymnastics

**Tony Murdock and
Nik Stuart**

**Foreword by
Elena Shoushounova**

Franklin Watts

London New York Toronto Sydney

Contents

© 1980, 1982, 1985, 1989 Franklin Watts Ltd
First published 1980
Revised Edition 1982
Revised enlarged Edition 1985
Revised Edition 1989
First published in Great Britain by
Franklin Watts Ltd
96 Leonard Street
London EC2
First published in the USA by
Franklin Watts Inc.
387 Park Avenue South
New York
N.Y. 10016
U.K. Edition ISBN:
0 86313 895-0
U.S. Edition ISBN:
0-531-10770-1
Library of Congress Catalog Card
Number 89-8870
Printed in Belgium

Acknowledgements

Jacket design: Edward Kinsey
Cover photo: Eileen Langsley/Supersport
Diagrams/design: Colin Ede
Photographs: Eileen Langsley/Supersport except the following:
BAGA: 28
Alan E. Burrows: 34, 37, 52, 70, 88
Paul Fender: 85
Foto-call: 99*t*
Pete Huggins: 98
Peter Moeller: 99*b*
Mervyn Rees: 2
Mark Shearman: 8
USSR Federation/BAGA: 69

Foreword

The sport of Gymnastics has given me both pleasure and great enjoyment in spite of the hard work and endless hours of training that are required to succeed. It has also given me the opportunity to travel the world, and in many countries meet their gymnasts and, of course, the public, who enjoy watching this very special and beautiful sport of ours.

I hope that both the girls and the boys who read this book will gain inspiration from its contents. May the detailed practical advice and the examples of the champions pictured in the book serve as stepping stones to a successful and enjoyable career in gymnastics.

Shoushounova Elena

Olympic Champion

Introduction

This book has been written to help aspiring young gymnasts who are thinking of taking up the sport or who have just started beginners' classes. We hope too that it will stimulate parents and teachers to take an interest in the sport and perhaps go on to become club coaches. We have tried to give as much practical advice as possible on preparation work and training to take the reader from the most basic movements to more advanced exercises on the apparatus for both boys and girls. The step-by-step illustrations make this a book which can be used both as a coaching aid and for reference, but we hope that it will be of interest to spectators as well as the gymnasts themselves.

Gymnastics is a sport for people of all ages to enjoy. The younger you start the better. You may never become an Olympic contender, but you can learn and get just as much enjoyment from your chosen sport as any international gymnast. Most boys and girls start their training between the ages of eight and ten years, although some, of course, begin much earlier.

Above Young gymnasts performing a floor exercise during a large schools' competition.

Below A class of young gymnasts receiving expert help from a trained coach.

Left Gymnastics owes a great deal to Olga Korbut for its rapid growth. Her performance on TV made almost every young girl in the world want to become a gymnast.

Below left Lisa Elliott, who became British National Champion for the third successive time in 1988.

Below right Valeri Luikin USSR, the Olympic Team gold medallist, individual overall silver medallist and silver medallist on parallel bars and high bar at the Seoul Olympics in 1988.

Bottom The USSR women's team after they had won the Olympic gold medal at Seoul in 1988.

2 Clothing and personal equipment

The most essential item of clothing for girls is a leotard. These are available in a wide variety of styles and shades and may be purchased in most department stores or sports shops. Leotards are also made for boys, but are usually only required for competitions. Boys wear shorts for the floor exercise, but where the legs come in contact with the bars or rings, long white trousers supported by braces or suspenders are advisable.

Tracksuits are a must for the warm-up. A well fitting suit is almost like a second skin, which should be removed when your body is warmed up and replaced when it starts to cool down.

Shoes are available in a variety of styles. Some gymnasts like to wear full shoes which are made of soft leather, while others prefer a half-shoe that covers only the front of the foot, leaving the heel bare. The shoe is attached round the back of the heel with an elastic strap.

Handguards are required to protect the gymnast's hands and give grip when working on the bars and rings. Handguards are made of soft leather and fit over the middle two fingers on both hands. They are fastened round the wrists with straps.

It is essential that long hair is tied back in a ponytail or bunches. Flying hair not only looks untidy but is dangerous for even the simplest of exercises.

Finally you will need a good strong-handled holdall or bag to carry your clothing and such additional items as resin to use on your shoes on slippery floors, hand chalk, wrist bandages, a tape measure, warm socks or leg warmers. All your clothing and training equipment should be kept clean and in good repair.

3 Safety

You must remember that not even the simplest exercises should be performed without supervision. It is most important that you work with a coach so that you learn the movements correctly from the start. Bad habits are difficult to break once they have been formed. There is also the possibility that you may hurt yourself if you train alone, and the more difficult the exercise, the more serious the injury is likely to be. So be sensible when you train and learn your sport safely.

Never work in the gymnasium alone and don't play the fool—it will usually lead to an accident. Make sure that there are plenty of mats and avoid slippery floors or surfaces that are wet. Do not work in poorly lit or restricted areas and don't leave tracksuits or clothing lying on the floor. Always check the equipment and apparatus before you start your exercises to make sure that it is secure.

Remove all jewelry and wristwatches before you start work and tie back long hair. Never chew gum or eat during your training. Don't try to work if you are unwell, for you will not be able to concentrate. If you are late for your session or class, don't cut short the warm-up. Complete it on your own and then join in. Having warmed up, don't sit around and get cold. Finally, listen to your coach or teacher—he or she *does* know what is best for you.

To summarize, here is a list of the ten most important safety rules:
1 Never train on your own.
2 Use plenty of floor mats.
3 Do not eat or chew while training.
4 Remove watches and jewelry.
5 Tie hair back firmly.
6 Check the apparatus before using it.
7 Do not work on slippery floors.
8 Do not try an exercise without help until you are sure of it.
9 Do not train when you are unwell.
10 Always warm up first.

4 Warming-up and conditioning

At the beginning of every training session you must first warm up your body. Warming-up does three things.

1 It increases the amount of oxygen in the lungs and therefore the supply to the muscles and joints.

2 It increases the flow of blood going to and from the various parts of the body and therefore the amount of energy.

3 It makes the mind more alert and so helps your co-ordination.

The warm-up should not be too long—ten to twenty minutes is ample in the early stages of training, although later you may need between one and two hours before a big competition.

A general warm-up

1 Running, hopping, skipping.

2 Leg swings forward, sideways and backward at the wall bars.

3 Standing astride, reaching forward and backward through the legs.

4 Sitting, rolling the legs back over the head and touching the ground behind.

5 Lying on your back and pressing up into the crab position several times.

6 Several forward rolls with the legs astride.

7 High tuck jumps across the gym.

8 Several cartwheels non-stop.

9 Sitting, straightening the legs to try to get the heels from the floor while maintaining contact with the backs of the legs.

10 Walking on the hands and turning on the hands.

Conditioning

Before you do any gymnastics it is important to realize that your body must be conditioned. Some people have better bodies for doing certain types of exercises than others. If you are very lucky, you may just have the right kind of body for all the exercises and will be able to perform them with little difficulty. However, if you are less than perfect, and most of us are, you would do well to prepare your body first with some conditioning exercises. The important qualities to develop in your exercises are as follows:

1 Tension

2 Range of movement or suppleness

3 Strength

4 Balance—especially on hands, but also on feet and other parts of the body

5 Endurance

Here is a series of exercises designed to improve all those five qualities to help you to become that most excellent of athletes—the gymnast.

Conditioning exercises

1 Crouch with your legs between your hands.

2 Stretch to standing with arms raised overhead, one leg to the rear.

3 Return to crouch.
Repeat 10-15 times.

1 Sit with legs forward, hands behind hips.

2 Slide hips forward and bend your knees until you are sitting on your heels.

3 Return to the long-sitting position.
Repeat 10-15 times.

1 Stand with arms stretched to the side.
2 Swing one leg high and clap hands together underneath it.
3 Return to standing position with arms to the side.
Repeat 10-15 times with each leg.

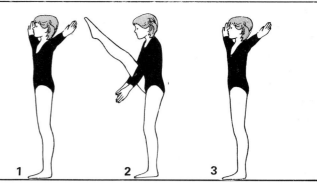

1 Stand erect.
2 Bend forward with legs straight and place hands on the floor.
3 Walk forward with the hands until you are in a V position.
4 Lower your hips until you are in a straight front support. Return to the standing position by reversing the movements.
Repeat 5 times.

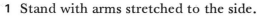

1 Sit on a chair with a straight body.
2 Grasp the seat and bend your legs up into your chest.
3 Straighten your legs until your feet are above your head.
4 Lower your legs.
Repeat 5-10 times.

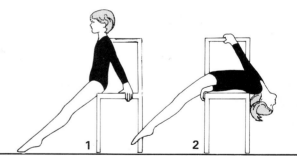

1 Sit across a chair, grasping the seat and back.
2 Lie back slowly until your body is fully extended.
3 Raise your body slowly until you reach the starting position.
Repeat 5-10 times.

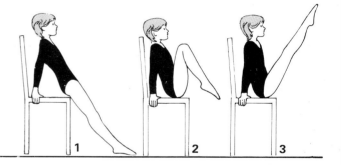

1 Grasp the seat and back of a chair, placing your right leg on the chair seat.
2 Bring your left leg between your hands to place it on the floor.
3 Return back over the chair starting with your left leg.
Repeat 15-20 times.

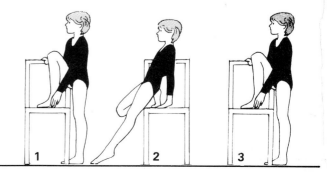

1 Stand erect with your right leg on a chair seat.
2 Bend sideways to touch your right foot with both hands.
3 Swing to the left to touch your left foot with both hands.
Repeat 15-20 times.

Hold your ankles and rock backward and forward. Repeat 10-15 times.

1 Sit with legs straight.
2 Roll slowly backward until your toes touch the ground behind your head. Keep pushing at the ground with your hands.
3 Roll slowly forward to the sitting position.
Repeat 5-10 times.

1 Get into a front support with straight arms.
2 Bend first one arm, then the other to arrive at the position shown in 3.
4 Straighten one arm, then the other to return to the starting position.
Repeat 5-10 times.

Skip for five minutes, varying the foot positions, hopping on one foot and then on two.

5 The floor exercise

The floor exercise area is 12 m square (each side is 39 ft 4½ in). The area is covered by a mat, usually made up of squares or long strips, not more than 54 mm (2 in) thick. The floor exercise is performed by both girls and boys, but in competition there are differences in the rules.

The girls must perform an exercise of not less than one minute and not more than one minute thirty seconds. The exercise must include balances, dance movements, acrobatics, turns, jumps landing in balance, and the whole routine should be ballet-like with continuous flowing movements. The gymnast must cover the entire floor area, so her routine uses the sides as well as the diagonals.

The boys' exercise is judged on more explosive acrobatics and stronger movements. The routine must include turns and balances and should show mobility, originality, steadiness in landing and elevation in jumps. The boys must use the whole area of the floor, touching each corner at least once. The minimum time for the exercise is fifty seconds and the maximum allowed seventy seconds. The boys' exercise is performed without music.

It is a good idea to include some dance training, preferably ballet, in your gymnastics. This will help you to learn to move gracefully and will improve your suppleness and balance. All ballet movements should be explained and taught by a qualified teacher, for you are likely to damage your feet, knees and ankles if you try to teach yourself.

Opposite Olga Bicherova, former world champion and the youngest girl ever to win a world title.

Below Vladimir Artemov, USSR Olympic Champion, Seoul 1988.

The basic techniques

The exercises that follow in this chapter are the basic movements of which the floor exercise is made up. When you have learned and perfected them, you will then be able to combine them into a routine. At the end of the chapter are two sample routines for girls and for boys.

We begin with three exercises that will prepare you for movements that follow.

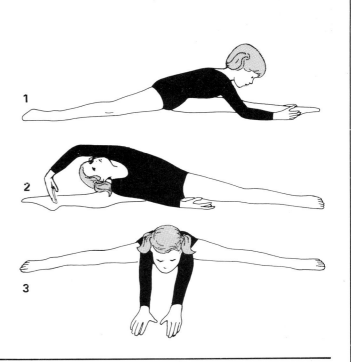

Preparation for the splits

1 Sit in straddle with your legs as wide apart as possible. Pull yourself down to the left and to the right.

2 Sit in straddle and reach over with your head towards your right ankle. Turn your body upward and keep your left arm above your head. Repeat the movement to the left.

3 Sit in straddle and stretch forward, keeping your back flat until your chest touches the floor.

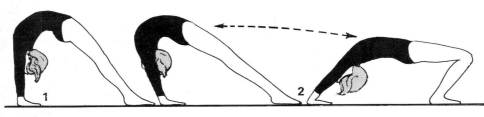

Preparation for the walkover

1 Get into the position shown, which is known as the back bend or crab. Keep your legs and arms straight.

2 Rock backward and forward in crab. Repeat ten to fifteen times.

3 Perform a back bend using a wall. Get your hands as far away from the wall as possible.

Preparation for forward folding

Using the beam, grasp the underside with your legs bent. Stretch to straighten your legs.

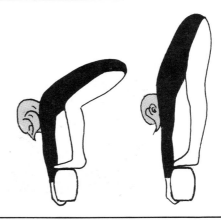

With a partner to help you, lean forward from a sitting position with legs straight and together. Your partner should hold your arms back with one hand at your elbows and one in the upper back. Don't round your back as you lean forward.

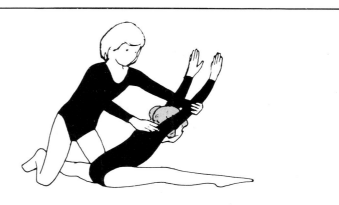

Sitting on the horse top, grasp the underside and pull down. Hold for thirty seconds and repeat ten times.

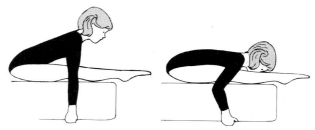

Daniela Silivas, Romania, will be best remembered for her epic battle with Elena Shushunova (USSR) in the 1988 Olympic Games in Seoul. Daniela won the overall silver and the gold in the individual titles on asymmetric bars, beam and floor, as well as a silver in the team event.

The handstand

The handstand is one of the most important movements in gymnastics. It is the basis for many other exercises on the vault, the beam, the rings and the bars. Learn it correctly from the start and you will be able to progress to the more difficult movements with confidence.

1 Stretch upward.
2 Step forward with your left or right leg. The rear leg will be the first to leave the ground. Bend your leading leg and push to swing your whole weight over your hands.
3 Keeping stretched, place your hands on the floor. Try to keep in a straight line from your hands to the toes of your swinging leg.
4 Now swing up into the balancing position.

Do not try to get your legs together until the first leg is upright.
5 Keep stretching upward without arching your back. Keep your legs tightly together with your weight on the base of your first two fingers. Your head should be in line with your arms, your arms touching your ears and your stomach muscles held tight. Don't hold your breath.

Remember, a good long step forward will give you more time to arrange yourself in the correct position of balance. Keep your body tense, but if you are straining then something is wrong. Look at the movements again. Your aim is to hold the handstand for ten seconds.

Improving the handstand

This exercise will help you get a straight line from hands to toes. It is important that your shoulders are flat.

good   bad   bad

The forearm balance

This is an excellent exercise for improving your hip movement, concentration and sense of balance. Incidentally it improves your digestion and general health, for it is a movement used in yoga.

    Place your hands as shown before putting your head in position. Your forearms will make a triangle, and most of the weight will be taken on your arms and the backs of your hands. Try it first on a soft mat. Later you will probably feel happier with a firmer surface under your arms, as this will enable you to obtain a good still balance position.

Lisa Grayson performing a floor exercise. British Asymmetric Bars Champion 1988, she is best remembered for the fact that she missed the plane to the Olympics in 1988 – when called up as reserve.

The headstand

Perform the headstand in the same way as for the forearm balance, but this time the hands and the head form the triangle, as shown here.

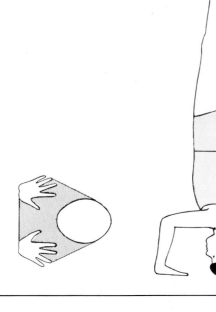

The forward roll

Start this exercise with a very soft mat.
1 Stretch your arms over your head, bending your legs.
2 Extend your legs. Try to cover about 1 m (3 ft) in the dive part of the roll.
3 Tuck your head in after placing your hands on the ground.
4 Round your back, bending your legs and roll on to your feet.

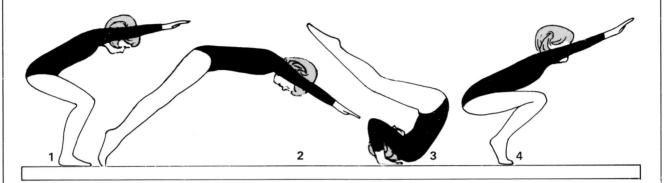

Preparation exercise for rolling

Stand on a soft mat, bend down and grasp your legs below your knees. Place your seat on the ground and rock backward on to your shoulders. Try to get back on to your feet after one or two rocking movements.

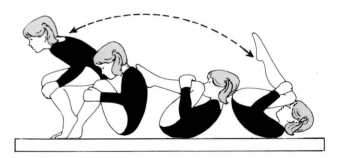

Place your hands behind your head and shoulders for this next exercise.
1 From a kneeling position on the box top, place your hands in the correct position. Bend slowly forward until you can reach the floor with your arms.
2 Push from the box top with your legs and toes. Roll forward to a sitting position.

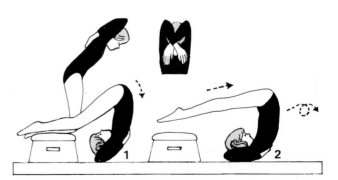

1 Try this movement with a partner standing between your legs, lifting them to waist-height. Keep your body tense and straight.
2 Keeping your arms straight, lift your seat as high as possible, pressing against your spotter's hands as you do so. Start to move your shoulders forward.
3 As your feet leave your spotter's hands, bend your arms and place your shoulders on the ground. Do not increase your hip angle. Roll forward.

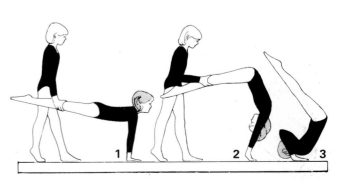

Rolling over a box top or bench is a very good way of improving your flight before the actual roll takes place. Do try to keep your head clear of the ground throughout the exercise and make sure that you have a good soft mat to land on with plenty of room in front, just in case you travel further forward than you thought you would.

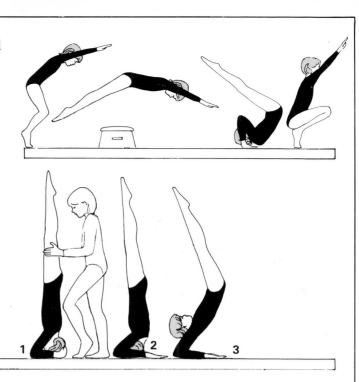

Rolling forward from the forearm stand with the aid of a spotter is the first stage of rolling down from the handstand.
1 Go into the forearm stand.
2 Push your shoulders back a little until you can lift your head off the floor.
3 Roll down, first to a sitting position, then to a crouch stand or into another roll.

Rolling down from the handstand

1 From the handstand overbalance slightly.
2 Continue to overbalance and bend your arms, tucking your head in.
3 When your shoulders touch the mat, bend your legs and roll to crouch.
4 Keep your arms forward and your back rounded.
   This is a very important linking exercise if you want to construct a sequence of several movements.

Rolling down with straight arms

1 Get into as straight a position as possible with a spotter assisting you.
2 Keeping your back, shoulders and seat tense, lower your head and start to lose balance forward.
3 Continue to overbalance, making sure that your feet also move forward.
4 Try to make contact with the ground as smoothly as possible and continue to roll forward with only a slight bend in the hips.
5 When you get to this position, start to bend your legs, but keep your back rounded.
6 You are now in a position to buck up to handstand to try the exercise again.

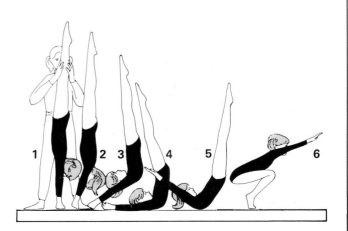

The backward roll

1 From a stretched position bend at your ankles, knees and hips.

2 Place your seat on the ground, bending your arms and placing your hands behind your head.

3-4 Roll backward, keeping your legs bent. Move smoothly from your shoulders on to your hands.

5 Push strongly from your hands to keep the movement going.

6 Finish in the crouch position.

1 Try this exercise on a springboard covered by a soft mat. Sit on the springy end with your hands behind your head.

2 Roll backward down the hill made by the springboard.

3 Keeping your legs bent, finish in a kneeling position. The slight slope will make the movement easier.

1 From a sitting position with the legs straight, the exercise is only a little more difficult, but the flat surface requires more effort from you. Perform the exercise on a soft mat to start with.

2 A tighter tucked position will help you to get over the top. Try to relax during the roll if it feels uncomfortable.

3 Finish in a kneeling position.

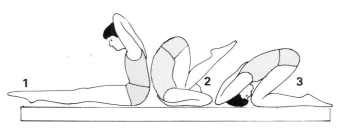

Backward roll with straight legs

1 Stand with legs well astride and bend forward.

2 Reach through your legs, at the same time losing your balance backward.

3 When your seat touches the ground, move your hands back behind your head and close your legs, keeping them straight.

4 Push with your hands and bend your legs to enable you to reach the crouch position on your toes.

This exercise is essentially the same as the one before, but it requires a deeper fold to get the hands well behind your heels. Do not bend your legs as you fall backward to touch the ground with your hands. Just try to get your thighs to meet your chest at 2, and you will find yourself rolling smoothly and easily on to your feet.

Try to imagine your feet are describing the line shown in the illustration. A much stronger thrust should be made with the hands than in the previous rolls you have attempted. Stretch the body fully when you reach the handstand position and do make sure that your spotter knows exactly what you are aiming to do.

Oksana Omeliantchic, USSR, joint World Champion in 1985. Suffered injuries in both the World Championship in 1988 and the Olympic Games in the same year. She was a unique performer in the floor exercises.

The approach run for the agilities

In gymnastics there is a special kind of run-in to the handspring, cartwheel and round-off —the movements known as the agilities. You must master this if you want to be a confident gymnast. You can learn the run quite easily if you follow the instructions below.

1 Assume a good stance, with your stomach muscles drawn in, your shoulders down and your weight on your toes.

2 Allow your body to fall forward as you step forward with your right leg.

3 Step forward with the left leg and lift your arms behind you.

4 Step forward with the right leg and swing your arms downward and forward.

5 Stretch the right leg and swing your arms upward. Both legs should now be stretched.

6 Land on your right leg, stretch forward with your left leg and reach forward with your arms.

This movement is known as the hop-step. You can reverse the movement if you prefer to take off from the other leg.

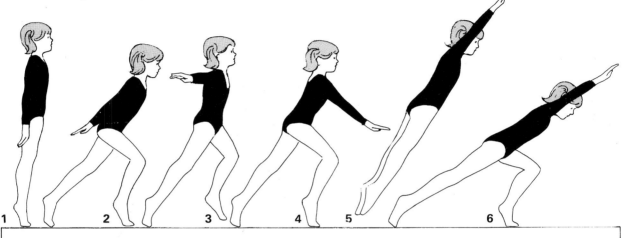

Now try the approach run again, adding a forward roll on to the movement. A spring-board will help you to improve your flight and give you more time to feel the rhythm of the exercise.

The handspring

1 Swing your arms upward and jump high with a slight forward lean to the body.
2 Step forward with the left leg.
3 Straighten the leg as your hands touch the floor.
4-5 Use lots of leg swing to get the elevation from the hands.

6 Keep your arms overhead as you land on one or two feet.
   Learn this movement on two feet at first. In this way if you do not manage sufficient thrust with the hands, you can turn your hips away from the forward direction and come down safely.

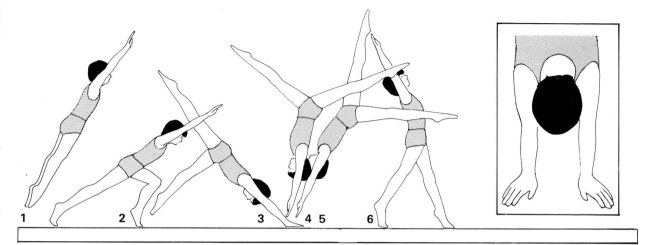

How to learn the handspring

1 Perform the handspring from three sections of the box with two spotters. Make sure there are plenty of thick mats to land on.
2 Keep your arms straight and use your

spotters all the way through.
Beware of moving your shoulders forward during the overswing. Keep your back straight.

h

Spotting for the handspring

1 Kneel at the side of the gymnast's path. Your left hand should support the shoulder.
2 Place the support hand as shown.
3 Your right hand supports the gymnast's seat.

Elevation practice

One of the most difficult things about the handspring is to lift into the air to give the impression that you are floating. This can only be achieved by getting the arms and trunk into a straight line before the thrust action occurs. A good way to get the feel of the thrust is to place a box top near the wall and swing up in a handstand to a position of 45 degrees. Keep your head well away from the wall throughout the movement. Do not try to go any higher than 45 degrees. If you do, you will not feel the essential lift action that will take you upward, allowing time for you to rotate and land on your feet. Push up from your shoulders and not from your elbows.

Start every session on the handspring with this exercise and you will soon see improvement.

Natalia Yurchenko, overall World Champion in 1984, considered to be the greatest classical gymnast ever produced by the USSR.

The backflip

1 Stand erect with arms raised overhead.
2 Bend your hips and knees, keeping your body erect and making sure that your knees remain behind your toes.
3 Fall backward and stretch your legs vigorously.
4-6 Maintain the extended position through to the handstand at 6.
7 Snap your legs down from your hips, thrusting strongly from your hands.
8 Land with a slight bend of your knees.

How to learn the backflip

1 Sit on the horse top with spotters positioned as shown.
2 Slowly at first, swing the trunk back into the stretched position.
3 Do not move your hands away from the horse but place them under your shoulders. Keep your legs straight as you come over and do not bend your arms.

Working with spotters

1 The gymnast stands erect between the spotters.
2 The spotters support while the gymnast swings backward on to the hands. The supporters must exercise great care and responsibility when assisting, taking all the weight of the body, allowing the gymnast to concentrate on the technique of the movement.

Learning the jump

1 From a standing position bend forward from the hips as shown. Your arms and the top half of your body should be parallel to the ground.
2 Swing your trunk backward by bending your knees until your arms are vertical and your thighs are parallel to the ground.
3 Push off strongly with your feet. Your toes should leave the ground last of all. Extend your hips, knees and ankles, keeping your head between your arms. Your arms should remain in line with your ears throughout the backward overswing. Try to keep your arms and head in this position when you bring your legs to the ground to prepare for your next backflip.

Constructing a routine

When you have learned and perfected the basic movements on the floor area, you will be able to put together combinations of the exercises to form a routine. Work with your teacher or coach who will give you advice on constructing your routine and your choice of music.

Draw up a list of all the exercises you can perform correctly. You will need to purchase or borrow a copy of the FIG (Féderation Internationale de Gymnastique) code of points, which lists the exercises in order of difficulty—A, B, C for boys and medium and superior movements for girls. Try to start and finish your routine with an exercise which is exciting and difficult, but which is within your capacity.

Draw out the pattern of your routine on a sheet of paper, aiming to use all the available space within the floor exercise area. If you are good at one type of exercise, try to make this the theme of your routine, but make sure that you achieve a good balance between jumping, suppling, strength and poise. The girls' exercise must flow like a dance to music, while the boys must display dynamic movements.

If you do stumble or fall, pick yourself up quickly and continue with as few unnecessary movements as possible. Remember that the finish of the exercise is the last thing that the judge sees, and it can have a definite effect on the score. Your pleasure at performing an exercise well will communicate itself to the judge if you stand erect and elegantly when you dismount from your routine.

Go through your routine until you know it perfectly and can perform it without thinking about the sequence of the exercises. You will then be able to concentrate on expressing each individual element at its highest level. Always try to perform with an audience, even if it is only one person. This will help you to get the feeling of a competition while you are training. Finally, remember that a simple routine performed well will gain more marks than a difficult routine performed badly.

Below Andrew Morris, the most stylish gymnast to emerge from Britain in recent years.

Opposite Marina Lobach, USSR Olympic Champion, performing with a ribbon in the Olympic Games in 1988.

A floor routine for girls

1 Extend your right leg sideways and raise your arms to shoulder-level. Lift your arms up and take your weight on your right leg, raising your left leg to the rear.

2 Hold your left leg with your left hand.

3 Step forward with your left leg, placing your right hand on the floor. Overswing (this is the tinsica) to stand on your right leg, stretching your arms up. Step forward with your left foot and swing through the handstand into a walkover on to your right leg. Swing your left leg down.

4 Continue to sink down into the splits.

5 Bring your left leg round to join your right leg. Reach forward to touch your toes.

6 Swing your legs strongly to bring yourself into the crab position. Stand erect.

7 Cross your left leg behind your right, circle your arms and turn left. Raise your arms and lift your left leg forward. Placing your left foot on the floor, spring high, extending your left arm sideways and your right arm forward. Land on your right leg and lower your arms to the rear. Step forward with your left foot and swing your right leg forward into a split leap.

8 Land on your right leg and step on to your left, raising your right arm and extending your left arm sideways. Place your right leg and your right arm forward. Pivot on your right foot with your left knee raised. Step forward with your left foot and swing to . . .

9 The handstand. Roll down forward to stand.

10 Taking one pace forward with your arms raised in front, swing your arms down and back. Swing into a back handspring. Place your right foot on the floor and make a half turn to bring your legs together.

11 Swing your arms to the rear, bending your legs. Forward roll. Continue with a headspring (or a forward walkover if you prefer) to stand with your arms raised.

12 Step forward with your right leg, extending your left arm forward at shoulder-level and your right arm up. With a quarter turn to the left, bring your arms to your sides and draw your left leg to the right to stand erect.

Opposite Melissa Marlowe, one of the rising stars of the US gymnastics squad, about to start her floor routine.

A floor routine for boys

1 Stand to attention. Take two paces forward and handspring to stand with arms raised.

2 Step forward with your left leg and lower your body forward into a horizontal stand. Hold for one second.

3 Place your hands forward and swing to handstand. Hold for one second.

4 Bend your arms and roll down to hollow front support. Place your right elbow under your hip and lever to balance on your right elbow.

5 Lower your feet to the floor and straighten your arms.

6 Pike sharply and bring your feet in to your hands. Stand erect with arms raised. Lower your arms to the side and turn on your left foot. Run forward into a round-off followed by a high jump with stretched body. Bend your legs as you land.

7 Make a high jump-turn with arms raised. Roll backward through to the handstand. Hold for one second. Place your right foot on the floor and turn left, extending your arms overhead.

8 Cartwheel to handstand. Snap your legs down to the floor and follow this with a backflip.

9 Jump and turn to your left to stand with arms raised forward. Circle your hands inward and stretch your arms forward and up. Kick to handstand. Hold for one second.

10 Roll forward and extend your right leg. Make a half turn to stand astride with arms to the side.

11 Lunge to the left, circling your arms down and then up to stand with arms stretched overhead. Circle your arms inward and bend your knees, extending your arms sideways. Straighten your legs and raise your arms forward.

12 Swing your arms downward in a complete circle and jump to handstand. Snap your legs down to the floor and straighten your body. Raise your arms up and sideways. Bend your knees and extend your arms sideways as you land. Straighten your legs and lower your arms to your sides.

6 The vault

The vault apparatus for girls

The vaulting apparatus is known as the vaulting horse. The height of the horse can be adjusted up to a maximum of 120 cm (47¼ in) for senior gymnasts, and to a minimum of 110 cm (43⁵⁄₁₆ in) for juniors under organized competition rules. The maximum length of the vault is 163 cm (64 in). It is covered in smooth leather or leather-type material. The vault is placed broadside so that the gymnast vaults over the width.

The run-up is 24 m (79 ft) in length, although for girls there is no maximum length. A girl can start her run as far back as she likes. However, vaulters such as Svetlana Boginskaia and Daniela Silivas have a starting point well within this distance.

A springboard is placed in front of the vault to give the gymnast 'lift-off' for the first flight on to the vaulting horse. The landing is made on to padded mats approximately 10 cm (4 in) thick with a non-slip surface.

There are twenty-six numbered vaults in the International Code of Points book. The value of these vaults are from nine to a full ten marks.

When a new vault is invented and performed, it is usually given the name of the person who perfected it. Most vaults are named after Japanese gymnasts, such as Yamashita and Tsukahara.

Girl gymnasts are allowed to have two vaults. The gymnasts may perform two of the same type of vault or two completely different ones. In either case the highest score will count.

Japanese competitor Yamashita was the man who changed the style of vaulting. He is seen here going into a cartwheel vault.

The vault apparatus for boys

The vault exercise for boys is similar to that for girls. The names of the vaults are the same, but the scoring values are different.

The vaulting horse is turned 90 degrees to the angle for girls. In other words the boys vault over the length of the horse instead of the width. The run-up is limited to 20 m (65 ft 7 in). The height of the horse itself is raised to a maximum of 135 cm (53 in).

In boys' vaulting the gymnast is only permitted one attempt at the vault, which must be named before the vault is performed.

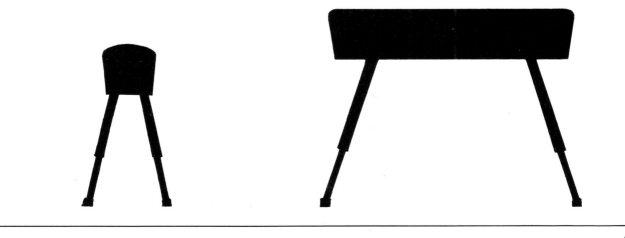

The vault exercise

Vaulting is the shortest exercise in the whole competitive field of gymnastics, and while it is true that you can get more points in less time here than anywhere else, you can also lose more.

Strong legs and a fast run are vitally important in vaulting, so work at skipping and running movements to help you develop a good consistent run-up to the horse. Always try to run in as straight a line as possible, if necessary drawing a mark with chalk from your starting point to the horse. Once you have developed a steady run-up, measure it out. This will save you much worry when you have to go to another gymnasium or perform away from your home ground.

At first you would be well advised to work in gym shoes or sneakers rather than bare feet. Place a mat over the springboard, and it will help you to avoid aching legs and lower ankles. To start with learn to jump and land over a line or bench, or even over a rope about 60 cm (2 ft) from the ground. Try to remain still on landing, without stepping forward and with only a slight knee-bend. Stretch your arms sideways as you land. Experiment with jumping down from different objects to get the feeling of landing without bending forward at the hips; this will help to strengthen the muscles used in the landing.

Perform all your early vaults over low objects and from a very short run. Three paces is a good distance to start with, and from there you can build up to a longer run. Always count your paces carefully until your stride length is regular and you can run twelve to fifteen paces, knowing for certain that you will hit the board on the last count. Try to keep your heels from slamming down as you hit the springboard, for this will slow your take-off and spoil your upward jump towards the horse.

Remember that the horse top is a booster platform for further elevation, not something to jump down from. Use your hands to push yourself into the air from the horse top with as much flight upward and forward as possible.

You can learn many of these things playing leapfrog with a partner, for the starting and the finishing positions are much the same in both elementary and advanced vaulting.

Never vault over objects that are wet, shiny or slippery. If you slip and fall, you are likely to damage your confidence as well as your self. Once lost it is hard to build up your confidence again.

The approach run

Before you start to vault, it is a good idea to spend some time developing your running technique. Your feet should be pointing straight to the front during the run, your arms swinging backward and forward and bent at the elbows. The arm action should maintain your balance and the rhythm of your run by working together with your legs. When your right arm is forward then your left leg should be forward, and when your left arm is forward, your right leg should be in front. This may sound odd, but it is probably the way that you run every day. Pick your knees well up and drive forward with your legs.

The take-off and landing

It is important to learn how to take off and land safely before starting to perform even the simplest vault.

1 Take a few running paces forward and as you jump upward and forward to the springboard, drop your arms behind you.

2 Swing your legs forward from the hips so that your feet strike the board well in front of the rest of your body.

3 Your body will now come into an upright position as you swing your arms forward very strongly.

4 When your arms are above your head and your legs straight, you will lift from the board. Emphasize the full stretch of your body at this point, for this is the first flight phase of the vault.

5 At the top of the jump bring your knees high up to your chest, keeping your arms forward and upward.

6 Now for the difficult part: stretch your body and legs straight before you land on the ground.

7 Land on your toes and stretch your arms forward with your legs slightly bent. Straighten your legs to stand up and move your arms sideways in line with your shoulders. Finally lower your arms to your side. The jump or vault is now considered complete.

This is a useful exercise to help you get the feel of the take-off and to land steadily. Use a springboard and the box top with one layer.

Emilia Eberle of Romania shows the approach flight into the Tsukahara vault. Notice that the turn is not yet complete.

Improving the landing

This exercise will help you to improve your landing and develop the second flight phase of the vault, known as the flight-off. Do not try this exercise from too high a horse. Start with the horse about waist-height; later you may wish to raise it to chest-height. Use a good deep landing mat for this exercise.

1 From a standing position on the horse, swing your arms and spring forward and upward, keeping your arms raised.

2 Stretch your body fully.

3 Feel your legs swing slightly forward in flight.

4 Now your legs are just in front of your body and ready to prevent any forward steps you might take.

5 Land on your toes, bending legs slightly with arms forward.

The front vault

1 Concentrate on your run, keeping on your toes, counting paces and swinging your arms.

2 Jump from about 1 m (3 ft) before the board, dropping the arms. Your feet should be in front of your hips.

3 Swing the arms and trunk forward to a near upright position.

4 Stretch your legs and lift arms above head-height.

5 Wait for the horse to arrive at your hands. Don't lean forward.

6 Bring your shoulders forward over your hands and swing your legs upward.

7 Start to move your weight on to your right hand.

8 Keeping your legs moving overhead, lift your left hand from the horse and continue turning.

9 Keep the turn going and look for the horse top all the time.

10 Bend your legs slightly and stretch your arms sideways. Recover to attention.

The flank vault

1 Check your run, keeping on your toes, counting your paces, swinging your arms.
2 Jump from about 1 m (3 ft) before the board, dropping your arms. Your feet should be in front of your hips.
3 Swing the arms and trunk forward to a near upright position.
4 Stretch the legs and lift your arms above head-height.
5 Wait for the horse to arrive at your hands. Don't lean forward.
6 Bend at the hips and swing your legs to the side, keeping your weight between your hands.
7 Lift your right hand, and as your feet pass over the horse, bring your hips forward in line with your legs.
8 Press forward on your left hand and keep the body straight.
9 Make sure your landing is directly in line with the springboard, for there is a tendency to move away to the right, or by leaning too heavily on the left hand to go to the left.

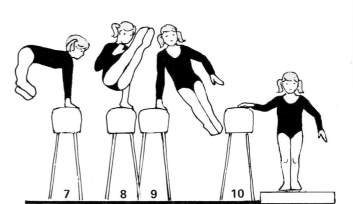

The rear vault

1-6 These positions are the same as for the flank vault.
7 After you have swung the legs to the side, continue to turn to the right.
8 Keep your hips piked and continue to turn, lifting your right hand off the horse. As you pass over the horse, reach back for it with your right hand pressing down firmly.
9 Extend your legs to the ground.
10 Keep one hand on the horse until you straighten your legs after landing, then lower your hands to your side and recover to attention.

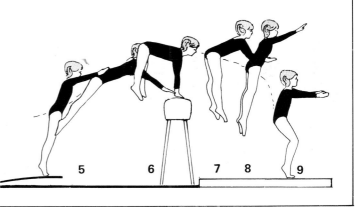

The straddle vault

1-4 As you will see by now, the run and take-off change very little.
5 Stretch your arms and reach for the horse with your hands well before your shoulders come over the top.
6 As your shoulders swing forward over your hands, lift your seat and open your legs for the start of the straddle action.
7 Push strongly with your hands as you pass over the horse.
8 Get into the flight position as soon as possible, for the longer you can show the straight flight position the better from the judges' point of view.
9 Keep the arms in front of the body, bending the knees slightly, and recover to stand.

The bent-legged squat

1-4 The approach run is as before.

5 As you can see here, the hands contact the horse later in the flight than in the previous vault.

6 Bring the knees well into the chest, keeping the toes pointed throughout.

7 Thrust strongly from the horse with your hands, striking downward with your legs and stretching them out.

8 Get into this position as soon as possible and hold it for as long as possible.

9 Bend the knees slightly and recover to attention.

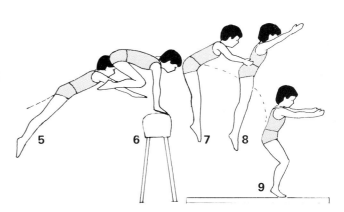

Li Ning from China is one of the greatest exponents of the vault exercise in the world.

The straight-legged squat

This vault may be performed by girls on the broad horse. Boys should try the vault first on the broad horse, and only when the horse is firmly fastened down.

1-5 The run-up and jump is as before.

6 Swing your legs high backward and upward to get them above your head before you start the squat action. The hands should be well in front of the shoulders when they strike the horse. The body should be almost parallel to the horse in the first flight phase. This is known as layout.

7 Move your shoulders forward as you begin the squat action.

8 Now make the squat, with the seat going higher than the head.

9 As you will soon realize, this action is not really a squat, for the hands are taken off the horse before the feet have a chance to get to the point where they would go through them. It is dangerous to try to keep your hands on the horse by leaning back and letting your feet get in front of your hips. Your head and feet must be in front of your hips when coming off the horse.

10 Get into the flight position, stretching your body, but don't arch your back.

11 Notice how the hips are slightly piked before the landing. This is important if you wish to learn how to land lightly from a fast-moving vault.

12 The longer horse will have made you stretch and run faster—therefore you will land with more speed than usual. With this vault there is a tendency to start slowing down when your hands touch the horse. . .DON'T!

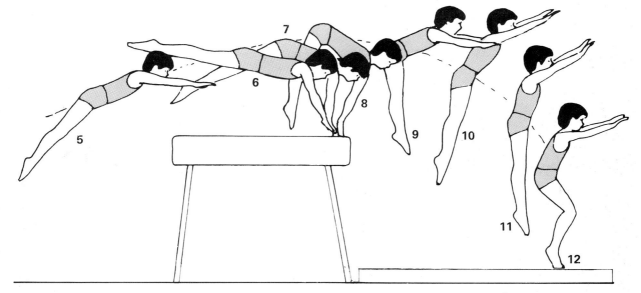

The straddle vault with layout

This vault is very similar to the straight-legged squat shown above, but the legs straddle the horse. The body should be almost parallel to the horse during the first flight phase—this is the layout.

The handspring vault

Girls should perform this vault on the broad horse.

1-4 Remember in this final vault the importance of the steady fast run-up, which is the key to becoming a top-class vaulter. Notice that the jump to the board is quite long but is also quite low.

5 The forward jump should be accompanied by a very strong arm-swing.

6 Although there is a slight pike in the hips, you should aim to get into a straight position as fast as possible.

7 As the hands strike the horse, the body is straight and ready to start swinging over the top through the handstand position.

8 The shoulders are forward as you reach the handstand position. Do not attempt to hold this position: it is just one element of the vault which should flow smoothly.

9-11 These three positions are in effect flying handstands. You will certainly need help from your coach at this stage, for if you are off course, you will not be able to see the ground until you have reached 11, and then it is too late to correct any fault.

12 It is important to have a rapid grasp of exactly where you are at the time you strike the ground. With practice you will learn to bring your head forward as you leave the horse and will be able to spot your landing position much earlier.

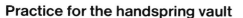

Practice for the handspring vault

This is a useful practice to improve your elevation from the horse, second flight phase and landing. Do not try this exercise without a spotter and a soft mat to land on. Make certain that your spotter knows how to stand in for the handspring on the ground, for the support needed is the same. The helper holds the gymnast on the upper arm and lower back.

This is a helpful practice for the overswing part of the vault (8-10).

7 Introduction to bar work

Bars are common to both male and female gymnastics. When you first start to use the bars, you must take particular care of your hands. Because you will train hard, sometimes on a single exercise, the skin of your hands can become worn or blistered. Always use handstraps to protect your palms. Blisters and sore hands will interrupt your training and therefore your progress.

However, if you do get blisters, treat them immediately. Remove the loose skin and wash the area in hot water. Apply an ointment that will prevent the skin drying and splitting. Very large blisters should be covered to keep them from the air for two to three days, when you will be able to remove the dead skin.

Use hand chalk at all times to give you a good grip on the bars. A light dusting is enough, or you will find that it goes into your eyes when you swing upside down. Always keep the bars free of caked chalk by wiping them with a damp rag.

Turn backwards

Heaves

Raise legs

8 The asymmetric bars

This apparatus is a development from the boys' parallel bars, which were once used by girls as part of their exercises. The change to high and low bar came in the early 1950s when the apparatus became a specially designed piece of equipment for girls.

The top bar is 2.3 m (90⁹⁄₁₆ in) from the floor and the lower bar 1.5 m (59¹⁄₁₆ in). Both bars can be adjusted up or down by 10 cm (4 in). The bars themselves are made of wood, and are 2.4 m (94½ in) wide. The distance between the two bars can be adjusted to suit the individual gymnast.

To begin her exercise the gymnast may mount the bars from either side. She may also use a springboard to start the routine. There is no set time for the exercise. However, most top-class gymnasts perform exercises for a period of about thirty seconds.

The requirements for a bar routine are swinging movements, changes in hand-holds, full use of both bars, and the whole exercise must have a flowing rhythm without any stops or hesitations.

Exercises on the asymmetric bars

The exercises on the asymmetric or uneven parallel bars are one of the most exciting parts of gymnastics to watch. They are also fun to perform, but only if you learn the correct basic elements. You will soon see that the exercises are mostly composed of swinging movements. The high bar is used for long swinging movements and the low bar for shorter swinging moves.

You will notice that even in the first exercise in this chapter both bars are used. This is to help familiarize you with the two bars. Although many exercises will be learned on one bar only, you must first make yourself 'at home' on both bars. Moving from one bar to the other is the key to all good routines and the exercises are planned to allow you to experience the use of the whole apparatus at a basic level. Good basics build champions!

Phoebe Mills, USA, bronze medallist on the asymmetric bars at the Olympic Games in Seoul 1988

Because of the nature of the apparatus you will be using your arm and shoulder muscles as well as your back and abdominal muscles. Strengthen these muscles by doing push-ups and sit-ups.

Push-ups using a chair

This exercise can be performed daily at home.
1 Hang straight without arching your back.
2 Bend your knees.
3 Stretch your legs and hold for three seconds.
4 Lower your legs and repeat ten times.

'V' sit-ups

A simple mount

1 Take a short run of a few paces from outside the ends of the bars.
2 Jump forward on to the springboard placed 30 cm (1 ft) from the bar uprights.
3 Grasp the low bar with one hand and spring to grasp the high bar with your other hand.
4 Keep your right arm straight and your legs to the rear as you prepare to swing forward.
5 Swing your legs forward and over the low bar to rest your seat on the low bar.

A simple turn

1 Follow the previous exercise to step 5. Bend your right leg and extend your left arm upward.
2 Start turning to the left and swing your right leg over your left.
3 Continue turning in the same direction with your left arm leading.

4 Keep your left and right legs strongly braced against the bars.
5 Swing your right leg between the bars and your left arm over your head.
6 Swing your right leg forward and bending it, place it on the low bar for balance.

From lying hang to straddle out

1 Hang from the high bar with your hips resting on the low bar. This is called the lying hang.

2 Raise your legs until your toes are level with your eyes.

3 Straddle your legs wide and swing backward.

4 Close your legs once you are clear of the low bar.

5 Hang fully stretched from the top bar.

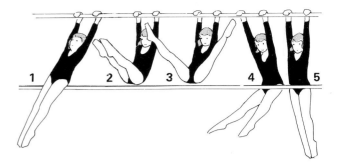

Leg-assisted upstart

1 Hang from the upper bar.

2 Place your right foot on the lower bar and raise your left leg over the lower bar.

3 Raise your left leg to the upper bar, keeping it straight.

4 Swing your left leg down and push strongly with your right foot.

5 When both legs are straight, bring your hips up to the bar and your shoulders over it.

6 Swing your legs to the rear and stretch into front support.

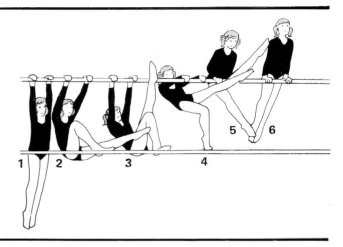

The upstart or kip

1 Start from a lying hang on the low bar.

2 Push your legs to the rear and your chest to the front.

3 Swing your shoulders back and allow your legs to swing forward.

4 Swing your legs to the upper bar before your shoulders have passed behind it.

5 Beat down with your legs and swing your hips up to the bar.

6 Bring your shoulders forward and swing your legs to the rear to maintain your balance.

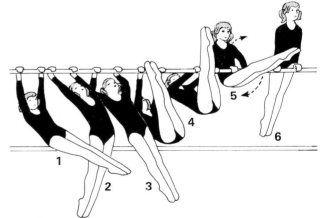

Leg-assisted rise from support

1 Support yourself with one leg bent over the bar.

2 Push backward until the back of your knee is crooked over the bar.

3 Lose your balance and swing backward with your arms straight.

4 Continue the swing right under the bar with your left leg straight.

5 Swing back up again pressing your left leg strongly backward to bring yourself up.

6 Rise above the bar to support by sliding the bar under your right thigh.

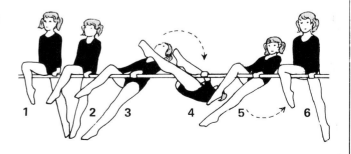

Leg-assisted rise from hang

1 Stand under the high bar and grasp the low bar.
2 Lean back on your arms and run forward under the low bar.
3 Continue until your shoulders are well past the low bar.
4 When you are at full stretch, bring your left leg up into the air.
5 Bring both legs together for an instant.

6 Swing your right leg between your hands, keeping your left leg straight.
7 Swing your left leg strongly down and backward, keeping it straight.
8 Push the back of your right knee at the bar and rise to support.
9 Slide your right thigh over the bar to maintain your balance.

Front vault with straight body

1 From front support in overgrasp on the low bar, swing your legs forward under the bar.
2 Keep your shoulders in front of the bar and swing your legs to the rear.
3 Turn your head and shoulders to the left and remove your right hand from the bar.
4 Keep turning your shoulders until you are sideways on to the bar and your legs are clear.
5 Change your grip while in flight to overgrasp again, and bend your legs slightly as you land.

Upward circle from standing

1 Stand at the low bar and grasp it with your arms bent.
2 Swing your left leg high toward the bar, pulling in with your arms.
3 Raise your right leg to meet the left, and keep the bar close to your body.
4 Pull hard until your hips touch the bar.
5 Lower your legs and lift your trunk. Keep your body straight when in support.

Upward circle from lying hang

This exercise uses the same technique as the previous one, but is a little more difficult.

Swing forward and turn to inside-sit

1 From cross support with legs to the rear, swing forward with your right arm straight, using your left arm to push your weight on to your right.

2 Swing your legs up and start to carry them to the right.

3 Swing your legs clear of the bar and keep turning to the right. Your right hand should be in front of your right shoulder.

4 Continue to turn, your feet following the direction of the arrow.

5 Keep your hips piked as you pivot.

6 Turn to front support on the low bar keeping your left hand on the top bar, or. . .

7 Continue to lift the legs and turn.

8 Sit on the low bar changing your grip on the high bar to overgrasp.

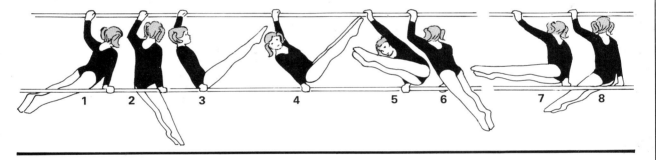

Front vault from low bar

1 Start in front support in overgrasp with your arms straight.

2 Swing your legs forward under the bar, but keep your shoulders in front of the bar so that you are angled at the hips.

3 Swing your legs backward, but not above bar-height.

4 Bend your legs and turn to the left.

5 Keep turning with your legs tucked and push off with your right hand, keeping your left arm straight.

6 Start to stretch your legs out for the ground, extending your right arm sideways.

7 Reverse the grasp of your left hand to overgrasp again. Bend your legs slightly as you land.

Opposite Brandy Johnson, seen here on the asymmetric bars. Brandy was a member of the US Olympic team in 1988.

Free hip circle to handstand

1 Swing up into a free horizontal support.
2-3 Swing your feet forward from the hips and push your shoulders back behind the bar.
4 This position can then be held and the swing stimulated by keeping the hips away from the bar. Your knees should be level with the bar.
5 Start to extend the hips and the shoulders. Push your toes straight up towards the ceiling.

6 At this point there is often a tendency to arch the back. Avoid this at all costs by keeping your stomach muscles tight and your legs stretched.
7 When the body is straight, it must be slightly behind the bar to ensure that you swing down the correct side of the bar and do not fall over backward.

Cast to upstart

1 Start from the position shown with your body extended over the bar in a V.
2 Tighten your seat muscles, straighten your back and press your arms down to your hips, bringing away from the bar.
Keeping your body straight, bring your arms forward in preparation to grasp the bar again.

4 Angle your hips before you grasp the bar.
5 Grasp the bar. Keeping the arms straight, push back away from the bar while bringing your feet forward into a deeper pike.
6-7 Swing down keeping the hips piked.
8 With a good straight body position from hands to seat, swing forward through into hang.

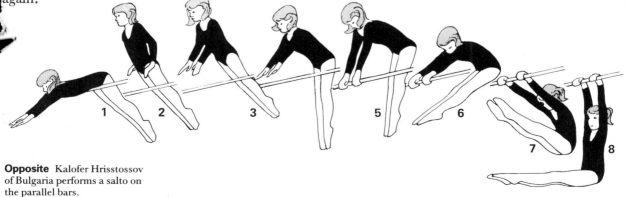

Opposite Kalofer Hrisstossov of Bulgaria performs a salto on the parallel bars.

Squat through to grasp the high bar

1-3 Stand under the high bar facing the low bar. Grasp the low bar and swing forward with a good stretch (2), before raising your legs (3).

4 Keeping your back as flat as possible, continue to raise your legs.

5 Bring your legs between your hands, making sure that you keep your ankles extended.

6 Continuing the backward swing, push your feet and legs through your hands.

7 Your shoulders should now be well above the bar, and the bar should be level with your hips.

8 Press your legs down, straightening out your hips and releasing your grasp.

9 Quickly take hold of the upper bar again in overgrasp.

10 The extension in the hips should now be complete and the arms straight. From here the shoulders can be brought forward to provide the starting position for an upstart.

Your coach should be standing alongside you to give you support under your hips and keep you moving to the upper bar.

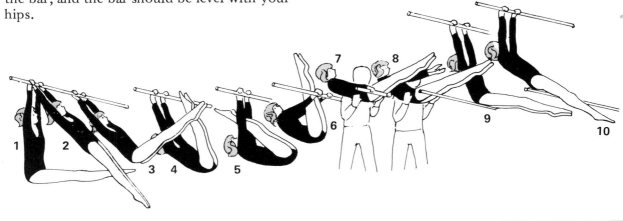

The upstart from low to high bar

1 Swing forward on the low bar in a good straight position from seat to hands, but with your hips angled.

2 At the end of the forward swing raise your legs to the bar.

3 Strike out with your legs as though for an upstart, but as your shoulders pass the bar, release your hold.

4 Quickly reach up with your hands for the high bar, keeping your body straight.

5 If you have kept your body straight, you will swing back correctly for the continuation to drop and catch the low bar.

Notice the position of the coach and the placing of the hands to support the gymnast under her hips.

Sole circle forward

1 With arms and legs locked straight, grasp the lower bar in an undergrasp, facing away from the upper bar.

2-3 Swing forward holding as deep a pike as possible through positions 2 and 3.

4 When your shoulders have risen above the low bar, you should lift your head to spot the high bar. Do not make the mistake of looking for the bar all the way round; wait until it comes into your vision.

5 Remove your hands from the low bar and reach up toward the upper bar, keeping your legs straight throughout.

6 Continue to press away from the lower bar.

7 Grasp the upper bar.

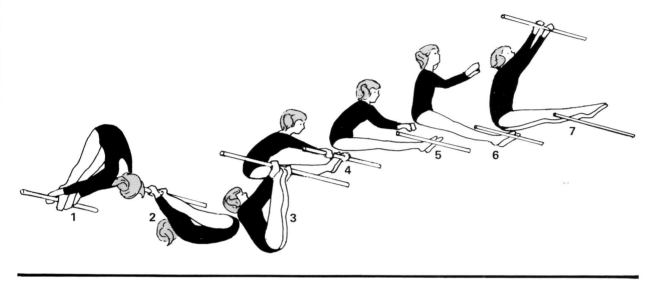

Sole circle and shoot

1 With feet and hands in contact with the low bar, face the upper bar.

2 Swing back with your legs and arms straight, pressing your feet strongly against the bar. Hold the fold position as deeply as possible.

3 When your shoulders pass under the bar, remove your feet from the lower bar.

4 Shoot your legs up toward the upper bar, pulling strongly on the low bar.

5 Press your chest through your hands, keeping your eyes fixed on the upper bar.

6 Transfer your grasp quickly from the low bar to the upper bar.

The whole movement depends on getting as much swing as possible in the first part of the movement and keeping it going until the catch is made.

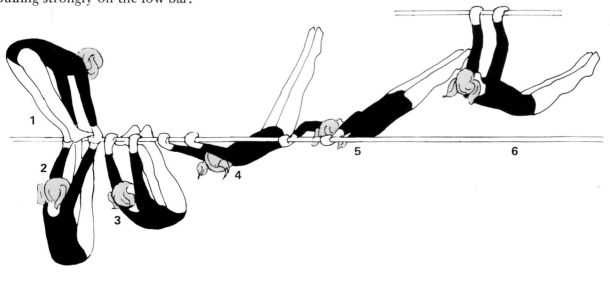

55

Hip circle forward

1 From an extended position on the low bar, face away from the upper bar.
2 Swing your trunk down forward with your arms straight out above your head.
3 Continue to swing, keeping your hips angled and your arms out in front.
4 Grasp the upper bar, trying to maintain the pike in your hips.
5 Swing your legs down and backward.

It is most important that you stretch your arms out fully at the start of the exercise before the hip pike begins.

Rear vault over the upper bar

1 Stand on the low bar with one hand grasping the upper bar in overgrasp.
2 Bend your arm and legs ready for the jump backward.
3 Spring backward, straightening your arms and legs and taking your weight on your right arm. Angle your hips by lifting your legs and keeping them straight.
4 Continue to hold the pike in the hips and swing your seat to the right, following the turn of your shoulders. Keep your left arm extended upward.
5 Extend your left arm sideways at shoulder-level and straighten your body, keeping the pressure on your right hand.

6 At this point it is important not to push with your right hand or you will overturn sideways with uncomfortable results. Drop and land as straight as you can, first making sure that there are plenty of soft mats.

Neck-spring dismount

1 Start in front support.
2 Swing your legs backward, and as you bend your arms, lift your hips.
3 Once the lift action is made, drop your head between your arms.
4 Place the back of your neck on the bar, keeping your hips well bent until this stage.
5 Start to press the legs away from the bar. This will increase the contact pressure at your neck and hands. Aim to take most of the pressure on your hands.
6 Press your legs outward until your body is straight. Continue to push with your hands until your arms are straight and your head is in line with your arms. Release your grip.
7 Try not to arch your back, but keep it straight so that you can spot your landing.

9 The parallel bars

The men's parallel bars call for swing, strength and a high degree of balance. The apparatus consists of a metal, weighted, free-standing frame with adjustable wooden parallel bars on top. The maximum height of the bars is 1.7 m (67 in) from the floor, but the height can be adjusted to suit any age group.

The exercise routine must include balances, showing combinations of strength and swings interspersed with holds in stationary positions of not less than one second. The entire exercise must flow smoothly from beginning to end. There is no time limit to the exercise, but most gymnasts work to approximately twenty seconds.

The bars themselves are made of a special type of wood, which when used properly can give you lots of spring into the air above the bars. Keep the bars free of grease and care for them as a violinist cares for his violin. Before you perform any exercises, wipe the bars with a damp rag. Rub the bars with sandpaper to keep them clean and smooth, removing all dust after you have done this.

Always check to see that the bars are set at the right width for you. This will probably be just a little wider than your shoulders, but you will find the correct distance by trial and experience. Never stand under the bars when you are adjusting the height. Always stand to the side, then if they do slip they will not crack you on the shoulders or head. Check that the clamp fittings are in the locked position and that the bars are not still on the small transport wheels that are sometimes built into the base. Use handstraps to protect your palms and plenty of mats to cushion your fall if you slip.

Andrew Morris, British overall champion for much of the 1980s, seen here performing on the parallel bars.

Strengthening exercises

Strength is a very important part of parallel-bar work. Use these exercises to develop your muscles.

1 Climb the rope using your arms only. Later try it with a weight of up to 4.5 kg (10 lb) on your feet. Climb 3 m (10 ft) of rope.

2 Perform push-ups with assistance in the handstand position on the low parallel bars.

3 Perform push-ups on the high bars with a weight on your feet. Only use the weights when you can do more than ten push-ups without them.

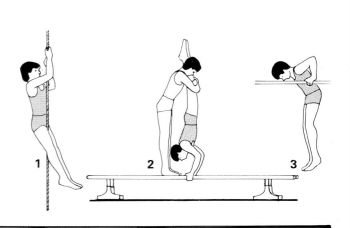

Swinging in straight-arm support

The swing in straight-arm support and the swing in upper-arm hang are the two most important exercises on the parallel bars. They are the basis for many other exercises, so you must master these two movements before you can really progress.

1 At the beginning of the forward swing, hold your body straight, your arms straight and keep your shoulders over your hands.
2 Move your shoulders slightly forward to keep your balance on the way down.
3 Your shoulders should now be over your hands.
4 Your shoulders should still be over your hands as you reach the upright position.
5 Now move your shoulders back to maintain balance as your legs swing upward.
6 The shoulders are now at the maximum backward lean.
7 Begin the backward swing, and start to straighten out your hips.
8 Start to move your shoulders back over your hands; your hips should be almost straight.
9 Your shoulders are now back over your hands and your body straight.
10 Swing, carrying your body back and upwards.
11 Your shoulders should be over your hands to provide the swing for the next forward movement.

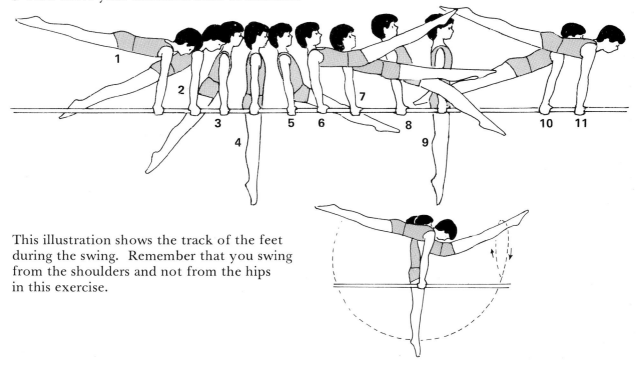

This illustration shows the track of the feet during the swing. Remember that you swing from the shoulders and not from the hips in this exercise.

Swinging in upper-arm hang

In this exercise the arms are stretched along the bars and therefore the swinging point is fixed at the shoulders. The strong part of the movement is the start of the swing. The hands should grasp the bar firmly.

1-3 Swing from your shoulders, keeping them in line with your hands.

4 Begin to sweep your legs upward, bending at the hips.

5 The angle at the hips is now at the maximum. Your hips should be at least level with the bars.

6 Begin to strike out your legs away from your hands to give momentum to the downward part of the swing.

7 This is the point where there will be the maximum pressure on your arms.

8 Your body is now straight and the swing upward begins. Pull hard on your hands at this point to keep your shoulders in the correct position.

9 The swing backward should be sufficient to carry your body above the bars.

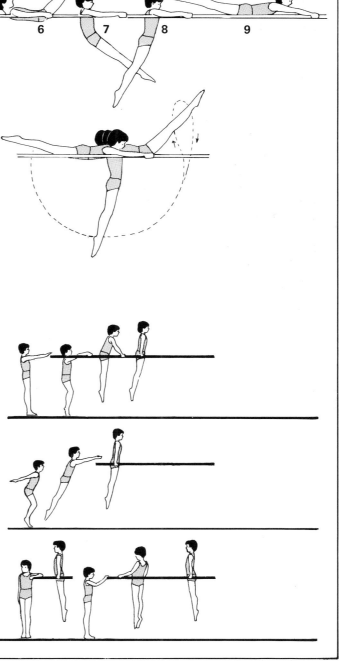

This illustration shows the path of the feet during the swing in upper-arm hang.

Exercises for the parallel bars

The exercises that follow start with simple swinging movements and progress to more complicated moves and dismounts. Each exercise is accompanied by a brief description rather than step-by-step instructions.

Stand at the end of the bars facing inward. This is known as a cross stand. Grasp the bars and jump up to support yourself with straight arms. Keep your body braced and very slightly arched to balance.

Taking a short run, spring to support on straight arms. Your elbows should be locked and turned very slightly outward. Keep your head in line with your trunk and your eyes fixed on the far end of the bars.

Stand at the end of the bars and spring to straight-arm support, making a quarter-turn or a half-turn. Make the turn after your feet have left the floor and not before you take off.

From cross stand facing inward, spring up and pass your right leg outside the right bar and under your right hand. You are now straddling both bars, supporting yourself at the rear. This position is called the cross-riding seat. Change your position to outside-riding seat by swinging your left leg over the right-hand bar.

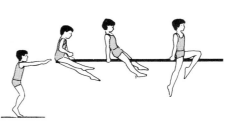

From cross stand facing inward, spring up and pass your right leg under your right hand to support yourself with your legs raised in front. Swing your legs to the rear, then swing them forward again to outside-riding seat on the left bar. Raise your legs to a half-lever position, hold for three seconds and dismount.

From cross stand, spring up to cross-riding seat grasping the bars in front of you. Keeping your body straight, move your hands to grasp the bars behind you.

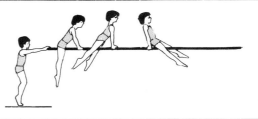

This exercise follows the previous one, but this time when you reach the end, raise your legs to the half-lever position. Hold for three seconds before lowering your legs to dismount.

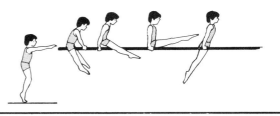

From cross stand facing inward, make a half circle with both legs over the right-hand bar, passing them underneath your right hand. When you reach cross support, swing your legs backward and dismount.

From cross stand facing inward, grasp the bars and spring up, placing your feet against the uprights of the bars. Bend your knees and then extend your legs so that you rise up to support.

From cross stand facing outward, undergrasp the ends of the bars as shown. Make an upward circle by bringing your legs right over until you can support yourself on both bars with your legs. Raise your arms over your head and return to cross support by closing your legs behind you.

From cross stand at the end of the bars facing inward, raise your arms over your head and bend forward. Circle your arms forward and grasp the outsides of the bars. Roll forward and as you come over, open your legs to straddle support. Remove your legs to go into cross support. In order to straddle the bars, you must bring your legs over strongly during the roll action in this exercise.

With your feet placed on the bases of the bars, grasp the ends as shown in the illustration. This is called the engaged grasp. Pull yourself up through bent-arm cross support to straight-arm support.

Stand outside the bars and grasp the near bar with your left hand in overgrasp and your right in undergrasp. This is called a combined grasp. Swing your legs over the far bar, briefly touching the bar with your back. Straddle your legs and turn, placing your left hand on the far bar. Close your legs and swing forward in upper-arm hang.

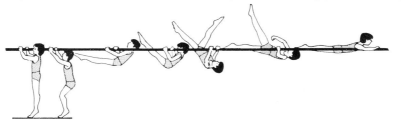

Stand outside the bars and grasp the near bar in combined grasp. Swing your legs up and over the outside of the near bar. Turn over the bar and support yourself in upper-arm hang between the bars.

Stand in front of the bars and grasp the far bar in overgrasp. Make an upward circle over the far bar with your legs and support yourself in the position shown.

Stand in front of the bars and grasp the near bar in overgrasp. Spring and place your feet in contact with the far bar. Keeping your arms straight, bend your legs and swing to support yourself on the near bar. Remove your legs from the bar when your body approaches the support position.

Stand in front of the bars with a combined grasp, your right hand in undergrasp. Swing up and over the bar in a flank vault, making a quarter-turn so that you reach cross support between the bars.

Stand in front of the bars and grasp the near bar in overgrasp. Bend your legs and straddle hop over the near bar to support yourself on the far bar.

Stand in front of the bars and grasp the near bar in overgrasp. Spring lightly and bend your left leg over the far bar. Bend your arms to bring yourself up to the starting position for the swing. Transfer your grasp to the far bar and circle right under and over the far bar until you are in support. Change to the cross-riding seat, grasping the bars in front.

Simple dismounts

Swing forward on straight arms and dismount forward as shown.

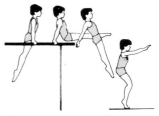

Swing on straight arms and at the end of the forward swing make a rear vault over the right-hand bar to dismount.

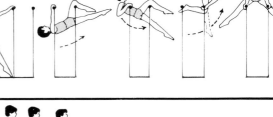
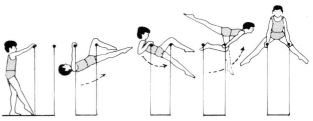

From the half-lever position, lower your legs. In bent-arm support overswing and dismount from the end of the bars.

From swinging in straight-arm support, pike deeply at the hips and underswing as shown to dismount forward at the end of the bars.

Swing on straight arms, and at the end of the backswing perform a front vault over the right-hand bar to dismount.

10 The high bar

The men's high bar or horizontal bar is probably the most spectacular of all their apparatus. The high bar is 2.4 m (94½ in) wide and 2.55 m (100 in) above floor level. The entire structure is made of steel.

During a routine the gymnast must produce swinging movements with changes of direction and changes of grip, including at least one cross-over hand-change. There is no time limit for the exercise, but most gymnasts work to approximately fifteen seconds.

Peter Vidmar was one of the most talented gymnasts ever produced by the United States. The content of his high bar exercise was superior to most gymnasts in the world.

You will see that many of the illustrations in this chapter show the low bar in use. In fact most of the more difficult exercises can be prepared first on the low bar. If you cannot do your exercises on the low bar, it would be foolish to try them on the high bar. Use handstraps from the start to protect your palms. A build-up of chalk on the bar will cause blisters, so keep the bar clean with sandpaper.

Hanging from the bar

It is important that you learn how to hang correctly from the start.

1 Hang from the bar with hands shoulder-width apart.

2 Your body should be in a straight line from hands to toes.

3 Beware of arching your back. This is a poor position and should be avoided.

The circle up

1 Grasp the bar at chest-height with your left leg forward under the bar and your right toe lightly touching the ground behind you.

2 Swing your right leg through under the bar.

3 Continue to swing the right leg forward and upward. Your left leg stays put.

4 As your right leg draws near to the bar, swing your left leg up to join it.

5 Keeping your arms bent, bring your hips up against the bar.

6 Keep your legs swinging over until you are in a V over the bar.

7 Keeping your feet still, lift your back and straighten your arms to support.

Remember that all high-bar work involves circling movements, so repeat this exercise until you can perform it smoothly without bumping your hips on to the bar.

The free circle up

1 Grasp the bar at chest-height, keeping your arms straight, your body erect and your right foot to the rear.
2 Swing your right foot forward and lean backward to prepare for the swing.
3 Bring both legs together and swing them vigorously upward.
4-5 Continue to swing with your arms straight.
6 As the swing begins to die, bend your arms as though you were pulling the bar toward your chest.

7 Now comes the tricky bit: you must rotate your hands around the bar from the hang position to a pushing position. This is called the snap-change.
8 By pressing at the bar with your hands, lower your hips to the bar.
9 Try to prevent your legs from dropping and your hips piking by tensing your seat muscles and stretching your legs.

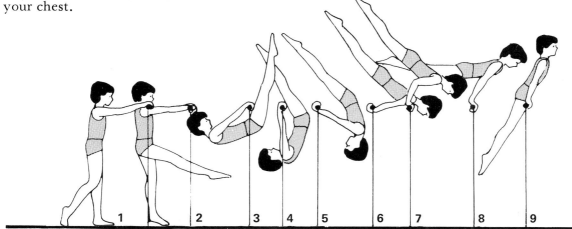

Free hip circle into hanging

1 From a hip support, swing your body backward until it is horizontal, keeping your shoulders over the bar.
2 As your legs start to move forward, swing your shoulders backward to increase the swing.
3 Strongly swing your legs through this position.
4 Your legs should now be almost touching the bar just above your knees.
5 Swing under the bar on straight arms with your legs moving strongly.

6 Push your legs and body away from the bar, holding your head forward.
7 Now comes the snap-change of the hands. Keep your body straight.
8 Keep your elbows in and continue to push at the bar.
9 Now straighten your arms. Be careful not to pike at your hips and shoulders.
10 Notice how little change of position there is between 9 and 10. Just stretch!
11 Swing down to hang.

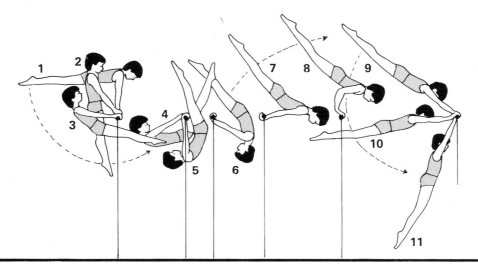

The swing

We can go no further until the swing has been mastered. Grasp the bar in an overgrasp with your thumbs going round the bar and touching the tips of your fingers. As you swing forward, hold the bar tight and don't let your grip rotate. Bend your wrists, but as you swing back, allow the bar to slide in your grasp.

Do not try to swing too high at the beginning. Start with a swing of about 45 degrees back and front. Once you have the technique under control, you can swing to a horizontal position. At the end of each backswing you will have to make a regrasping action as your hands unwind.

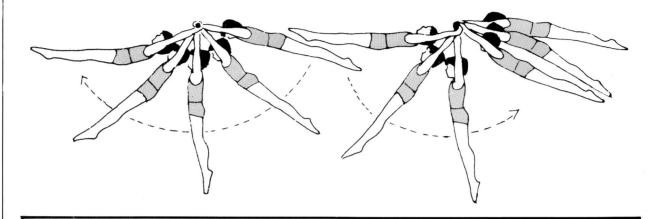

Forward-jump dismount

1 From front support swing your legs forward under the bar.
2-3 Swing your legs backward and at the end of the backswing bend your knees.
4 Place your feet on the bar between your hands.
5 Stretch your legs straight and lift your arms upward and forward.
6 This stretch position should be bold and emphasized.
7 Swing your legs forward to prepare for the landing. It is important that you pike your hips.
8 Bend your knees slightly as you land. Try the landing on a soft mat at first. Then move on to a good firm mat to ensure that your legs strengthen up for the dismount from the high bar.

Squat one leg through

1 Swing your legs forward.
2 Swing your legs backward, but not higher than the bar.
3 Keeping your shoulders forward, bend one leg into your chest.
4 Pass this leg over the bar, keeping your shoulders forward.
5 When your leg has cleared the bar, bring your shoulders back over the bar to keep your balance. Stretch both legs.

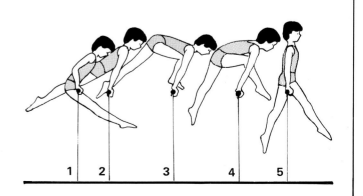

Squat both legs through

1 Swing your legs forward under the bar.
2-3 Swing your legs to the rear, but not as high as the bar, and start to lift your knees.
4 Continue to lift your knees right into your chest, keeping your shoulders in front of the bar.
5-6 When your feet have passed over the bar, move your shoulders backward as your feet and legs move forward to balance.

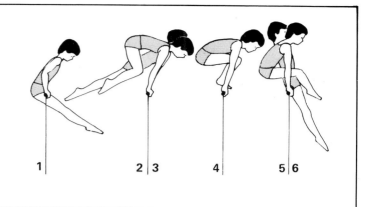

Sole circle backward

1 From a standing position on the low bar, grasp the bar with your hands either side of your feet.
2-3 Swing backward with legs and arms straight and your feet pushing hard against the bar.
4 When your hips pass the uprights, bend your legs to speed up the circling action.

5-6 Keep pulling at the bar, even though your legs are bent.
7 This is the important part: the snap-change takes place now as you bring your seat back over the bar.
8-9 When you feel balanced on top of the bar, you can if you wish straighten your legs and arms fully and go into a second circle.

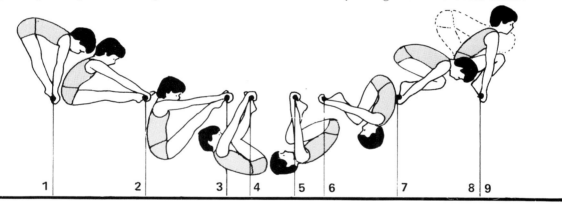

The upstart

1-2 Swing forward with your body straight and stretched.
3 Start to lift your legs at the end of the forward swing.
4 Continue lifting your legs, but do not bend your arms.
5 Your legs should now be lifted high until your ankles are level with the bar.
6 Now start to swing your shoulders and body backward, at the same time striking out for the ceiling with your feet to help speed up the backswing.
7-8 Keeping the backward swing going strongly, try to hold the bar close to your thighs all the way up.
9 Swing your trunk forward to get your weight over the bar and swing your legs backward to obtain a balanced position on straight arms.

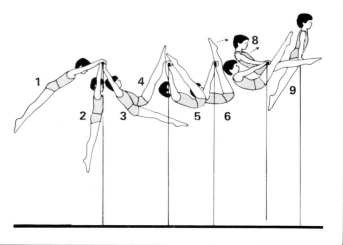

Starting the swing from hang

1 Hang from the high bar in overgrasp, with your thumbs round the bar touching your fingertips.
2 Raise your legs forward until they are parallel to the ground.
3 Swing your legs backward and push your chest forward.
4 Swing your legs forward again and your shoulders will move backward.
5 Shoot your legs away from the bar, pressing with your hands.
6 Continue to extend until your chest comes to the fore and your body is straight.

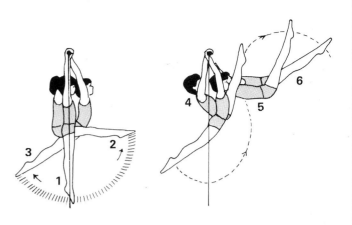

Shoot to back support

1 Swing forward.
2 Continue to swing strongly.
3 Lift your legs at the end of the forward swing.
4 Carry your legs up higher than the bar, keeping your arms and legs straight.
5 At the end of the forward swing place your feet between your hands and under the bar.
6 As the backward swing starts, stretch your legs out from the hips.
7 Carry on stretching until you reach the back-support position. Keep your balance in the back support.

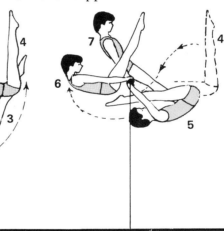

Squat in and shoot over the bar

This exercise is a development from the previous one and continues from stage 5.
1 As you reach the end of the backward swing, push your feet strongly toward the ceiling and press on the bar with straight arms.
2 Continue pushing your hips and feet through. This is the point of most force.
3 Your shoulders should still be behind the bar as your hips pass over the top.
4 Move your hips forward and upward away from the bar.
5 Now your shoulders pass in front of the bar as your feet continue to rise.
6 Extend your hips to thrust yourself forward. Pike slightly before you attempt to land.
7 Land on your toes and bend your legs.

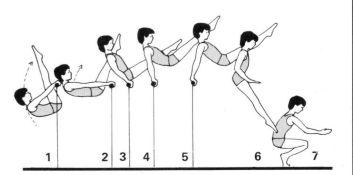

Opposite East German star Holger Behrendt performs a one-armed giant during his high bar exercise.

68

11 The rings

The rings exercise is performed by men only. The rings are suspended 2.5 m (98½ in) above floor level. The rings themselves are made of wood and are attached to canvas straps which hang from steel wires. The wires are attached to the ceiling of the gymnasium or to a rings frame.

Most gymnasts are helped up to their first hold by their coach. The routine must include swinging exercises with at least two handstands held steady for a minimum of two seconds. The dismount can be either forward or backward, and the gymnast must be balanced on landing if he is not to have points deducted. There is no time limit for the exercise, but most gymnasts work to a routine of between thirty and fifty seconds.

The exercises in this chapter are primarily swinging movements. When you first start to use the rings, swinging with a good range of movement will be your first aim. However, no matter how well you can swing, you will also have to include some very strong still positions like the cross, half-lever and the planch. These require very strong shoulder muscles, so do not neglect the strengthening exercises.

Keep the rings free of chalk using sandpaper or a damp rag. If the rings are new, remove the varnish with sandpaper.

Opposite Lou Yun of China, one of the greatest exponents of the ring exercise.

Above Dimitri Bilozerchev, USSR, one of the greatest male gymnasts the world has ever known. In 1985 at the age of 16 years he won the World Championship, retaining it in 1987. In 1988 he returned to gymnastics after a very serious car accident, and won an Olympic gold medal in the team event.

Strengthening exercises and still positions

1 With a helper holding your ankles and lifting most of your weight at the beginning, raise and lower from support through to the position shown.

2 This is good training for the crucifix position and will strengthen your shoulders. Place your hands through the ropes or straps, and laying the rings flat on the forearm, lift your feet from the floor.

3 Using the box and rings as shown, try to hold the position with the minimum of support from your legs on the box.

4 Using two sets of elastic expanders, press down with straight arms. Keep the rings at shoulder-height for six seconds. Repeat six times.

Pull to support

Try this exercise at first with a partner lifting your legs. The movement requires great strength, but you must learn to pull rapidly to be able to change from a hanging position to a supporting one.

The half-lever

Support yourself with straight arms with your legs parallel to the ground, keeping the rings absolutely still. You can perform this move on two chair seats put together, but not on the backs of the chairs!

Back planch

Get an old bicycle tire, cut it, and attach the two ends to each of the rings with string. Holding the rings, place your feet in the tire, keeping it taut, and turn upside down. You will then be able to lower to the position shown with little trouble. Repeat six to ten times. It is better to go into the correct position several times than struggle to do it badly without the help of the rubber tire.

Front planch

Perform this exercise in exactly the same way as the back planch. Then try to do one after the other, first to the front, then swinging the legs straight back to the rear.

Crucifix or cross

Again using the bicycle tire, lower to the full cross position several times. Later you will be able to tie these last three positions together, just as you have seen the world's best gymnasts do in competition.

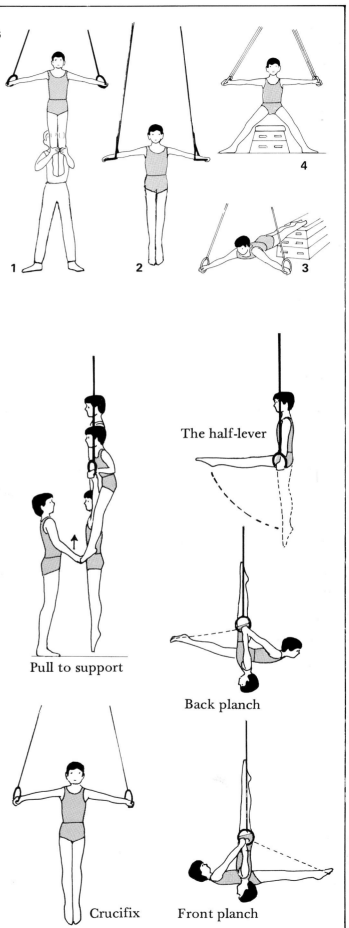

1   2   3   4

Pull to support

The half-lever

Back planch

Crucifix   Front planch

Balancing exercises

Your spotter should hold the rings very still even if you fall over.

1 Bring your shoulders forward.
2 Bring your legs up.
3 Pull your shoulders back and keep your body straight.

Swinging in hang

1 At the beginning of the forward swing your body should be stretched, but do not arch your lower back.
2 Continue to swing down forward and you will feel your body straightening.
3 When you reach the vertical position, stretch to really feel the bottom of the swing.
4 Lift your legs forward at a slightly faster speed than your swing.
5-6 Bend your arms and pull the rings into your shoulders and in line with your eyes.
7 Straighten your arms *before* your feet have a chance to fall down below your shoulders —this is very important.

8-9 As you begin to make the backward swing, you must think of unrolling so that the swing down occurs in this way: first arms straighten; second hips reach the bottom of the swing; third feet reach the bottom of the swing. In this way you will soon be able to swing down with momentum to take you from one movement into the next. This action can be seen in the illustration at 7, 8 and 9.
10 This is the continuation of the backward swing, which is assisted by pressing the hands forward.

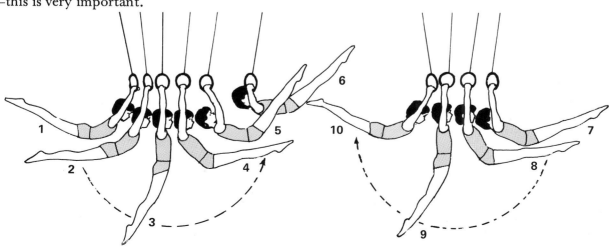

A strength exercise

1 Turn to an inverted hang.
2 Bend at your hips and lower your legs.
3 Continue to stretch out until you are in a back hang with your body as straight as possible.
4 Lift your seat up again until it is higher than your head.
5 Now swing your legs up until you are straight from head to toe.
6 Continue lifting with a straight body until you are back to your starting position.

The idea of this exercise is to keep the body as straight as possible as you lift back to the starting position. You will see that this relates to the back part of the exercise called the inlocation. The exercise will also strengthen your muscles to help you to perform the upstart.

The inlocation

Remember that this is a swinging exercise and not a wriggling one!
1 Push the rings as far back as possible at the forward end of the swing.
2 Swing back, and as your heels rise above your shoulder-level, push the rings sideways to help your feet to keep moving upward.
3 As your feet start to slow down at the end of the backward swing, lift your hips and pike strongly. As you do the pike, the rings will come back into the straight position.
4 Continue to rotate forward until your arms and your knees are in contact. From here you can repeat the exercise. Three times will be enough at the start.

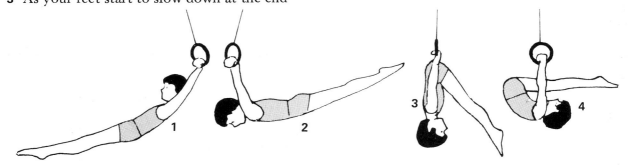

Ian Shelley, Great Britain, who trains in the USA, became Champion of Great Britain in 1988 at Wembley.

The upstart forward

1 Start in an inverted hang.
2-3 Lower your legs down to your chest.
4 Swing your legs out away from your chest.
5-7 After your legs have passed the line of the ropes, bend your arms and pull through the rings to a support position. Get into the support position before your feet drop below the rings.

8-9 Lower your legs to the straight position. Keep the ropes away from your arms, not only to prevent rope burns, but also because marks are deducted in competition if the arms make contact with the ropes.

The fly-away dismount

1 Swing forward and over the top. Your feet should pass through the rings before you extend the body for the dismount. When you have mastered this dismount, move on to stage 2.
2 This time extend your body before your feet pass through the rings. Dismount, keeping your body stretched all the time.

The straddle dismount backward

1 Push the rings forward as you swing down with your body stretched.
2 Keep swinging in full extension.
3 Push your seat into the swing with your chest leading.
4 Lift your legs by bending at the hips.
5 Bend your arms and start to straddle your legs.

6 Keep pulling on your arms and continue to bend them.
7 Stretch at the hips and release the rings when you have no more rotation left.
8 Extend the hips fully and open your arms.
9 Land on your toes and bend your legs slightly. Recover to attention.

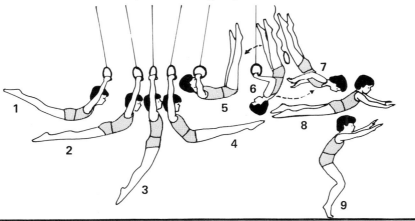

The dislocation

Although the exercise is called the dislocation, it is really a rotation of the shoulders. Do some arm circles and then, standing at the low rings, imitate the exercise as closely as you can, but keep your feet on the floor all the time.

1 Start in an inverted hang. Look at your toes and keep your head forward.

2 Slowly bend at the hips.

3 Bring your legs right down to your chest.

4 Drive your legs up for the ceiling.

5 Press your arms sideways as though you were going into a swallow dive and lift your trunk.

6 Keep your body fully stretched and reach forward with straight arms. Keep a tight grasp on the rings.

7 Reach for the floor with your feet and release the rings.

8 Bend your knees on landing.

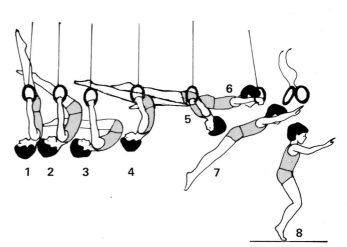

Circle up to support from standing

1 Grasp the rings with your arms bent and your right leg to the rear.

2 Swing your right leg forward, keeping your arms bent.

3 Push off with your left leg, but keep your right leg swinging upward.

4 Bring both legs together, bending your arms all the time.

5 Now for the hard part: still bending your arms, bring your body up and over the rings.

6 Push hard at the rings to prevent your body falling through.

7 Lift your trunk and assume the straight position shown.

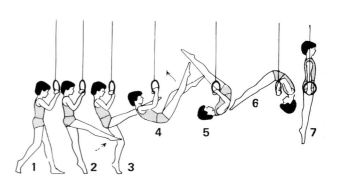

Circle up to support from swinging

1 Swing forward with your body stretched.

2 Swing, but do not pull back on the rings.

3 Try to 'bottom' the swing before you start to lift your legs.

4 Start to swing your legs upward, bending at your hips.

5 Pull at the rings and bend your arms strongly.

6 You are now over the rings. Keep them close to your hips.

7 With the rings at your hips, allow your legs to swing down. Keep the rings close together.

8 Hold your body straight, resting your full weight on the rings with your arms clear of the ropes.

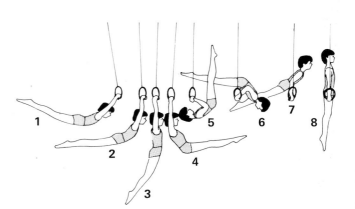

12 The beam

The beam is the only true piece of apparatus developed for girls. It is 5 m (16ft 4⅞ in) long and 10 cm (4 in) wide. For girls below the age of fifteen years it is 110 cm (43⁵⁄₁₆ in) above the level of the floor, and for girls over fifteen the height is 120 cm (47¼ in). The beam is made of laminated wood and covered in chamois to give the gymnast grip on the surface.

The exercise has a maximum time limit of one minute thirty-five seconds and a minimum time limit of one minute fifteen seconds. During the exercise the gymnast must produce walking steps, running steps, balances, jumps, leaps, 360-degree turns, high and low poses, and the whole exercise must flow smoothly.

Mary Lou Retton who became the first gymnast from the USA to win the Olympic overall title in 1984.

The gymnast first learns to perform a beam exercise on a line drawn on the floor. She then progresses to a low beam, rising by steps until she is working at the full height.

To learn the exercises correctly you must first fix this sequence of apparatus in your mind.

1 Floor line   Easier to learn on
2 Bench   To get the feel
3 Low beam   To get used to the width
4 High bench   To get used to the height
5 High beam   To get ready for competition

With all the exercises shown in this chapter use this sequence of apparatus to improve your confidence and skill. As a general rule start low and increase the height gradually.

Balance is, of course, the most important aspect of beam exercises. A slack body is difficult to control. The way to make balance work easier is to develop body tension. Stretch upwards and you will feel how much easier it is to do even the simplest everyday movements of walking, turning, sitting and running. This stretching or extending action is basically what body tension is all about. You can improve your body tension by doing some simple exercises.

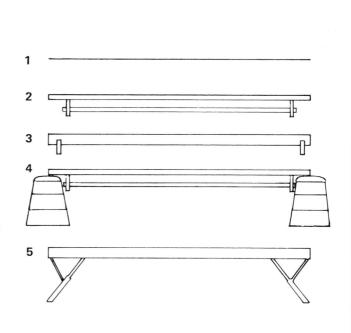

Exercises to develop body tension

1 Lie on your back with your legs bent and your arms stretched above your head.
2 Stretch your legs, but keep your body flat on the floor, especially your lower back.
3 Bend your knees up again and repeat ten times.
4 Beware of arching your back and allowing light to show through here. Ask a friend to check this for you.

1 Get up into a straight handstand with your body facing away from the wall. Flatten your body, stretch fully and hold for ten seconds. Your hands should be about 10 cm (4 in) from the wall.
2 Climb backward up the wall getting closer to the straight position with each attempt. When you can reach the straight position, increase the length of time of the hold. Make sure that the wall is smooth and that there are no projections to catch yourself on if you should slip sideways.
3 This is the finished position with maximum extension.

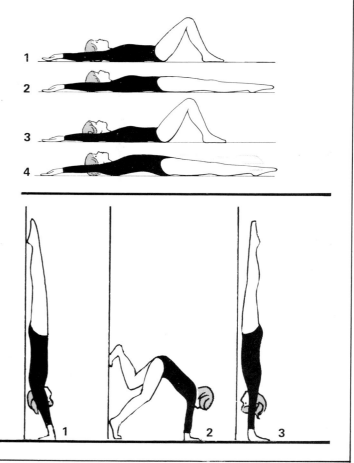

Position of feet and hands

Accuracy of footwork is of the greatest importance when working on the beam, for the width is only 10 cm (4 in). There are several ways to place the feet. You will soon come across all of these, but positions 1, 2 and 3 are the ones to concentrate on with the weight on the ball of the foot over the centre of the beam.

You should also know how to position your hands. Balance across the beam with your hands placed as in illustration 1, and balance along the beam with your hands positioned as in illustration 2.

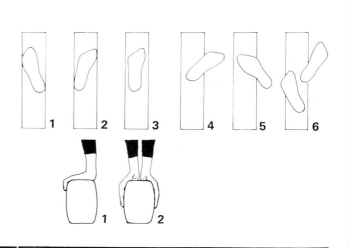

Exercises on the beam

You will notice in the exercises that follow that we begin with dismounts. It is very important that you should learn how to get off the beam correctly and safely from the very start. As you progress to more difficult exercises, you must be well used to correcting your position in mid-air in order to land steadily on your feet.

Karen Hargate was a member of the British team at the Olympic Games in Seoul in 1988.

Dismounts: the straddle jump

1 Stand on your toes with your arms stretched out sideways.
2 Swing your arms down, bending your legs.
3 Stretch your legs and swing your arms upward as you jump from the beam.
4 At the height of the jump straddle your legs and bring your hands down to your toes.
5 Extend your hips and swing your arms overhead.
6 Bring your legs together and show the flight position.
7 Bend your knees as you land on your toes and recover to attention.

Take care not to lean backward as you make the jump. Press your legs down to the ground as you straighten out, but do not throw your trunk backward.

The piked-jump dismount

1 Stand on your toes, then bend your knees as you swing your arms backward.
2 Swing your arms up and make a good strong jump upward and forward.
3 Bring your hands and feet together to touch your toes.
4 Straighten out at hips and shoulders.
5 Show the flight position.
6 Bend at ankles, knees and hips and recover to attention.

The handstand dismount

This is a useful dismount to follow a cartwheel.
1 Start from a straight handstand position.
2 Push with your right hand, bring your head through in line with your trunk and over-swing.
3 Push strongly with your left hand and stretch your right arm out straight.
4 Look down to spot your landing point, but do not bend at the hips or drop your head forward.
5 Concentrate on straightening out before you actually touch down, then bend your legs and land on your toes.

The squat-jump dismount

1 Stand on your toes, extending your arms sideways to balance.
2 Swing your arms down and bend your legs.
3 Swing your arms upward and jump with straight legs and a slight forward lean.
4 Bring your knees up to your chest and grasp them with your hands just below your knees.
5 Drop your legs while still in flight, but don't hold on to them after you start to descend.
6 Stretch out, showing the flight position.
7 Bend and recover to attention.

Mounts: to kneeling

1 Stand to one side of the beam on a spring-board and place your hands on the beam about 15 cm (6 in) apart.
2 Jump up to support yourself on your hands and swing your left leg to the side until it touches the surface of the beam.
3 Turn with your weight supported on your hands and the toes of your left foot.
4 Raise your hips and place your right knee on the beam. Bring your hands together with the fingers pointing down the sides of the beam.

Mount to straddle

1 Stand on the springboard with your hands placed on the beam as before.
2 Jump to support, swinging your left leg to the side. This time your leg must clear the beam.
3 Start turning to the left with your weight on your hands and your legs straight.
4 Continue to turn until you are straddling the beam.
5 Bring your right hand back in line with your left hand.
6 Grasp the beam with your thighs and place your hands behind you to keep your balance.

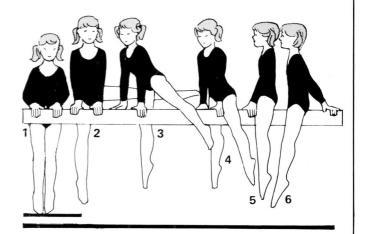

Mount to side-extended squat

When you have mastered the first two exercises, try this mount to a side-extended squat.
1 Stand at the beam as in the previous exercise.
2 Spring lightly, bending your right leg.

3 Place your toes on the beam between your hands.
4 Swing your left leg sideways, placing your foot on the beam.
5 Extend your arms sideways to balance.

A vault mount

1 Run up to the beam, placing your right foot on the springboard and your left hand on the beam.
2 Swing your left leg through, taking your weight on your left hand.
3 Place your left foot on the beam in front of your left hand, with your weight on your hand and toes.
4 Move your weight forward on to your left foot and begin to reach forward with your right leg.
5 Bring your arms forward and place your right heel on the beam with toes outstretched.

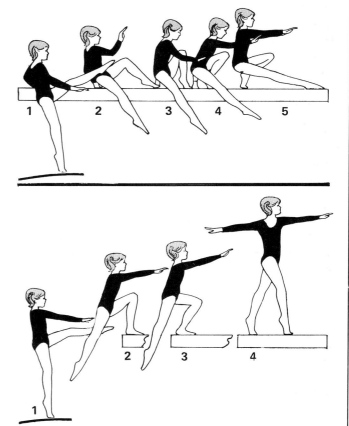

A jump mount

1 From a short run place your right foot on the springboard and swing your left leg up.
2 Keeping your arms forward, place your left foot on the beam with your knee bent.
3 Move your weight on to your left leg, stretching your right leg behind you.
4 Swing your right leg forward and straighten the left leg. Extend your left arm forward and the right arm back.

A forward-roll mount

Try this first on a bench covered with a mat.
1 Take a short run of two or three paces to the beam.
2 Place your hands on the beam.
3 Spring, lifting your hips high over your head.
4 Roll your head forward, tucking your chin right down on to your chest, placing your head on the beam as close to your hands as possible.
5 Keeping your legs straight and your back rounded, roll forward until your seat touches the beam.
6 Transfer your hands to behind your hips and keep your legs high in front of you.

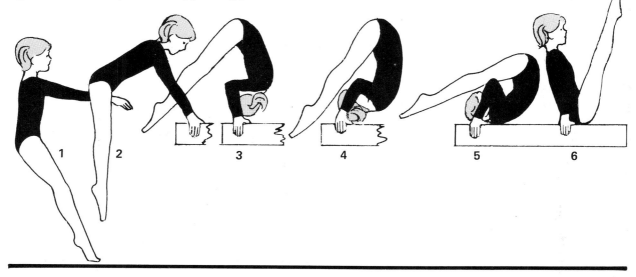

Movements on the beam: swinging in straddle

1 Sit astride the beam, raise your legs in front and place your hands forward.
2 Grasp the beam with both hands and start to swing your legs to the rear.
3 Continue to swing your legs to the rear, pushing down on your hands with arms straight.
4 Push hard on your hands and move your shoulders slightly forward in front of hands.
5 Let the swing carry your legs and hips away from the beam.
6 After your legs and hips have reached the top of the swing, bring your shoulders forward again and return to the straddle sitting position.

Swinging to knee support

1 Perform the swing as described above but with more leg lift. Do not bend your legs.
2 Tighten your seat muscles to get a better swing back.
3 Swing your legs back until they are parallel to the beam.
4 Keeping your right leg straight and high, bend your left knee, placing your toes down first on the beam.
5 Bend your left knee fully and hold your straight leg high with your head up.

Forward roll from straddle

1 Sit astride your arms with your hands on the beam.
2 Swing your legs backward, moving your shoulders forward.
3 Continue the swing until your legs are at an angle of 45 degrees to the beam.
4 Pike at the hips with your weight well forward on your hands.
5 Bend your arms, tuck your head in and place your shoulders on the beam. Slide your hands down the sides of the beam.
6 Grasp the beam firmly and pull your shoulders flat on to the beam as you unwind.

Backward roll to left-knee support

1 Lie flat on the beam, reach back and grasp the beam with both hands. Swing your legs overhead.
2 Place your right foot on the beam, toes down first, pressing down with your hands to protect your head.
3 Taking your weight on your toes, lift your head from the beam, keeping your left leg high.
4 Place your right knee in position, keeping your left leg stretched high and your head and shoulders up.

Jumps and springs: from two feet

Perform this exercise first on a bench or low beam.

1 Balance on your toes with feet side by side and arms held upward and forward.

2 Bend your legs, swinging your arms to the rear.

3 Stretch your legs as you swing your arms upward.

4 Jump at full stretch, keeping your eyes firmly on the beam.

5 Land on two feet, bringing your arms down and bending your knees.

6 Absorb the shock of landing and gain control by bending your knees fully with your arms back.

7 Straighten up to stand on your toes and keep your arms to the rear.

From one foot

Now try the exercise jumping from one foot to one foot. Again, try it first on a bench or low beam.

Spring with leg change

To begin with try this exercise without any forward movement. Keep your eyes on the end of the beam to help maintain your balance, but do not lower your head.

1 Stand on your toes with your left leg in front and your arms to the rear.

2 Spring up and swing your right leg in front of your left.

3 Now swing your left leg in front of your right.

4 Land on your toes with your left leg forward and your arms behind you.

5 Swing your arms forward and stretch your legs, keeping on your toes

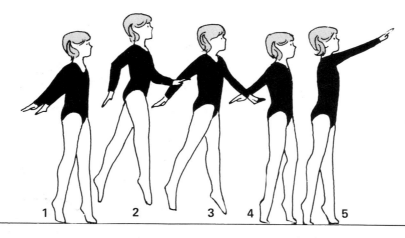

Gallop spring

Accuracy in landing is essential in this movement. Keep your eyes fixed on the beam all the time.

1 With your arms held to the rear, swing your left leg upward, bending it sharply.

2 As you spring into the air, bend your right leg and extend your left arm in front and your right behind you.

3 Stretch your left leg down for the beam.

4 Land on your left leg, keeping the arms elevated to shoulder-height.

Swing down from handstand

1 The movement starts from a fully extended handstand.

2 Move your shoulders forward, keeping your weight over your hands.

3-4 Swing down with your feet about 60 cm (2 ft) apart.

5 Swing your hips down to meet your hands and straddle the beam.

Natalia Shaposhnikova made the difficult lever to one-hand stand a feature of her routine on the beam. She is now a leading world judge of gymnastics.

The cartwheel

Keep your legs fully astride throughout this movement and do not allow your body to lean forward at the start or finish of the exercise, or you will lose your balance. You should be absolutely confident about performing a cartwheel in a straight line on the floor before attempting it on a bench or low beam.

1 Stand with your legs astride, arms extended and shoulders back.

2 Swing over on your left leg, placing your left hand on the beam. Keep your eyes on the beam.

3 Pivot sideways over your left arm, keeping the weight of your body over the left hand.

4 Place your right hand on the beam and transfer your weight on to it.

5 Place your left foot on the beam with your toes pointing towards your right hand.

6 Stand erect.

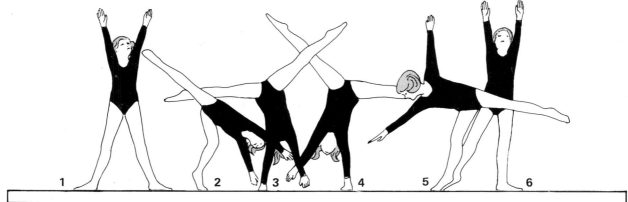

The forward walkover

Starting the walkover from a handstand is perhaps the best way to learn the movement, for it allows you to understand how your weight is transferred.

1 The movement begins with a vertical handstand.

2 As your legs come over, your shoulders move back so that your weight is maintained for as long as possible on your hands.

3 When your foot contacts the floor or beam, your shoulders, and therefore your body weight, is moved forward on to the supporting leg. This allows you to use the principle of the see-saw to reach the upright position.

4 Lower your right leg and stand erect.

The supporting leg should bend as little as possible at the beginning and should be completely straight at the finish. For the backward walkover simply reverse the movement.

Opposite Kelly Garrison Stevens, a member of the US Olympic team in Seoul, 1988.

13 The pommel horse

The pommel horse exercise is the scourge of male gymnastics. More Olympic and World Championship gold medals have been won or lost on the pommel horse than any other piece of apparatus. The horse used is the same as the vaulting horse, but curved wooden pommels are attached.

The exercise requires absolute and maximum concentration. The gymnast can mount the horse from either side, and once he begins the exercise he must produce flowing movements using all three sections of the pommel horse. At no time must any part of the body, except for the hands, touch any part of the apparatus.

There is no time limit for the exercise, but most gymnasts work to a routine of between thirty and forty seconds.

The pommel horse involves little danger —there is no height and therefore no fright! However, it demands that you pay particular attention to detail right from the moment you begin. In return it will give you immense satisfaction when you learn some movement that you had previously thought beyond your reach.

Opposite Vladimir Gogoladze, a member of the Soviet gold medal winning team at the 1988 Olympic Games in Seoul.

Below The Soviet gymnast Yuri Korolev demonstrates superb ability and technique on the pommel horse.

Preparation work for the pommel horse

Work on the pommel horse is very much like a series of continuous swinging vaults, so you will first have to learn the basic vaults correctly. Vaulting has already been covered in an earlier chapter, but here for reference are the two main vaults used on the pommel horse.

The flank vault

Jump up, getting your hips high in the air above your head. Take one hand off the horse and reach high with it. Extend your hips and swing sideways over the horse. Land with your back to the horse.

The front vault

Place both hands on the horse. Lift your hips up in line with your shoulders. Push hard with your right hand, turning your shoulders to the left. Keep your body straight for as long as possible as you pass over the horse. Land with your left side nearest to the horse.

The shear action is an important element of pommel-horse work. Learn the movement on the rings as shown, trying to get as much leg separation and angle in the hips as possible. Your foot should swing higher than your head. Swing only sideways and do not be tempted to bend your hips or bring the lower leg up to the higher one.

When you support yourself on the horse, stretch your arms and pull your stomach in, lifting your diaphragm. This helps you to keep well away from the horse when you are swinging round it.

It is useful in the early stages to work with a partner, helping one another to learn the correct movements. The spotter should stand to the rear and grasp the gymnast's ankle firmly as shown. This will enable him to perform movements with his other leg without rushing or interrupting the flow.

With the apparatus set up as shown, you will find it easier to learn the shears and circles. You can, if you wish, wrap foam rubber around the bars to protect your arms and so enable you to work for longer periods.

Exercises for the pommel horse

The exercises in this section are graded to enable you to learn and enjoy them as your skill increases. Eventually you will be able to string several exercises together to form a continuous routine. There are two important points to remember when you follow the descriptions that accompany the illustrations. Circling the legs to the right means moving them in a clockwise direction; circling to the left means moving them in an anticlockwise or counterclockwise direction.

Boris Schakhlin, renowned for his technical accuracy rather than acrobatic ability, performs a rear-in to saddle on the pommel horse. He is now a leading world judge of gymnastics.

Stand at the side of the horse, stretching out behind with the leg nearest to the horse. Swing this leg up high over the horse, trying to get the support arm straight as soon as possible. This is known as the oblique rear vault.

The next two exercises should be learned on the horse without pommels. Sit in straddle and swing your right leg back and then forward. Swing your left leg back and dismount to the right of the horse with a half-turn to your left.

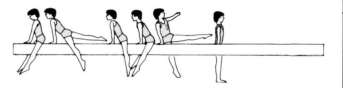

This exercise is designed to teach you the straddle walk. Place your right hand on the horse and swing your left leg forward across the horse. Place your left hand down on the horse in front of your left leg and swing your right leg back across the horse. Place your right hand on the horse in front of you and dismount to the left.

Start this exercise straddling the horse between the pommels (in the saddle) with your left leg in front. Turn to your left to straddle the end of the horse with your right leg forward. Circle your left leg forward over the horse, placing your right hand on the end of the horse, and dismount.

Start this exercise as before, straddling the horse and turning to the left. This time regrasp the pommel with your right hand and make a half circle to the left with your left leg. Keep working at this exercise until you can perform it smoothly.

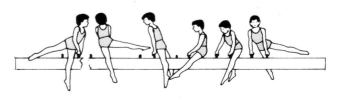

Sit in straddle, grasping the pommels in front of you with both hands. Make a full circle to the left with your right leg, lifting one hand at a time for your leg to pass over. Keep your arms straight throughout this exercise.

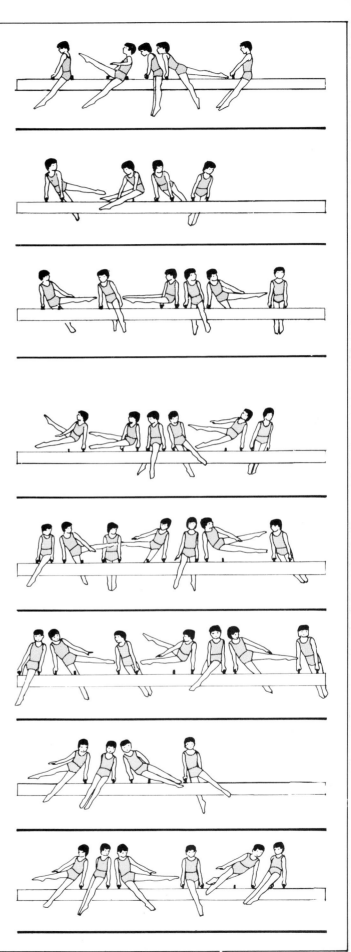

Spring up and swing your legs to straddle your left arm. Circle your left leg to the left until you are back in support in the saddle. Keep your left leg moving throughout the exercise and your arms straight. You are not allowed to rest your elbows on your hip bones!

Starting in support between the pommels, half circle your left leg to the right. Swing both legs to the right and half circle your left leg to the left, so that you are back in support. Try to achieve the maximum of swing in this exercise.

Spring up and half circle your left leg to the left so that you are straddling the horse. Release your right hand from the pommel as your left leg comes over. Now half circle your left leg to the right to come back to support. Try to swing high to the right so that the movement is like that of a pendulum rather than a circling of one leg.

Starting in straddle with your left leg forward, make a half circle to the left with your left leg, followed by a full circle to the left with your right leg. This exercise is a development of the previous one and again you should aim to swing like a pendulum.

Starting in straddle as before, half circle to the left with your left leg, and then continue with a full circle left. Lift your right leg high as you swing your left leg forward under your right hand.

Start in straddle with your left leg forward. Make a full circle to the left with your right leg. This is a useful exercise to help you learn to obtain separation and control in single-leg circling.

Start in back support as shown. Make a full circle to the left with your left leg. This is a similar exercise to the previous one and you must be definite about transferring your weight from one hand to the other.

This exercise illustrates a simple flank dismount from straddle support in saddle.

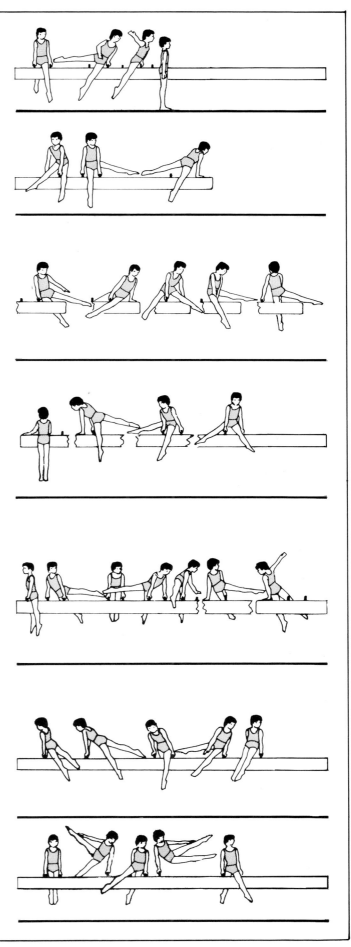

Start by straddling your left arm as shown. Make a full circle left with your left leg, finishing with a half-turn to the end of the horse.

Facing the end of the horse, grasp the left pommel with your right hand and place your left hand on the horse. Half circle right with your left leg and straddle turn on your right arm until you are able to grasp the pommel with your left hand to bring you into the saddle. This is a useful movement to take you from one section of the horse to the next.

Place your left hand on the horse and take hold of the left pommel with your right hand in a reverse grasp as shown. Spring up and make a full circle left with your right leg. The reverse grasp will enable you to turn as you come over the horse to finish straddling your right arm.

Starting by straddling the end of the horse, half circle left with your left leg. Half circle left with your right leg and without pause continue circling your right leg to dismount with your left hand on the end of the horse. It is important that you take all your weight on your left hand at this point in order to get well clear of the horse in the final part of the exercise.

Starting in support, make a full circle left with your right leg. As your right leg crosses the horse in the first half of the circle, your body turns too. For this to happen you must change your hands over as shown in the illustrations. This movement is sometimes called the simple Swiss turn; your trunk turns 180 degrees while one leg makes a full circle.

The illustrations here show the front shears to the left and right. Try to perform five on each side before moving on to the next exercise. Good shears shape a smooth routine on the pommel horse.

Next we come to the back shears. If you can perform three each side non-stop, you are well on the way to becoming a good pommel-horse gymnast.

From straddle with your left leg forward, half circle left with your right leg and swing both legs into a rear-vault dismount to the left.

Facing the end of the horse, place both hands on it. Flank vault over both hands to dismount with your back to the horse.

This exercise is a rear vault into the saddle. Push off from the end of the horse with your right hand, stretching your right arm as you pass over the horse and making sure that it is straight when you grasp the pommel. Stretch your body, but don't arch when you reach back support in the straddle.

This final exercise involves a full circle with both legs. Circling both legs is only possible when the arms are kept straight and the body and legs well clear of the horse. When your legs pass to the right of the horse, your shoulders should move to the left; and when your legs pass to the left, your shoulders should move to the right. Aim for maximum style by keeping your legs together and your toes pointed so that your body and legs swing as one unit.

Charles Lakes, one of the most spectacular performers on the high bar in the USA.

15 Sports acrobatics

Gymnastics sports acrobatics is exciting to watch and great fun to perform. It is rapidly rising to a leading position in television sports ratings and is becoming increasingly popular with clubs, for it requires no special equipment. It is certainly a very rewarding sport in terms of physical fitness and elegance.

At present the USSR teams are the best in the world, but the Chinese have a long history in the sport and some of their work is extremely original and highly entertaining. It is not yet included in the Olympics, but it has its own World Championships.

Most schools and gymnastics clubs will include sports acrobatics in classes for beginners. Many coaches will probably be willing to teach the elementary moves in the sport. There are, however, specialist clubs for the sport.

In Great Britain sports acrobatics is included in gymnastics and comes under the same ruling body, the British Amateur Gymnastics Association, but elsewhere in the world it is regarded as a completely separate sport.

Sports acrobatics is performed by both girls and boys and includes the following events:

Tumbling	boys
Tumbling	girls
Pairs	boys
Pairs	girls
Mixed pairs	boy and girl
Threes	girls
Fours	boys

The tumbling exercise is performed on a strip 20 m (65 ft) long and 2 m (6 ft) wide. For most gymnasts this will be the ordinary gymnastic floor mats, but top performers in competitions use a specially designed sprung runway made of laminated wood. This acts like a springboard to enable the gymnast to perform complicated twists, double and triple somersaults or flips.

Both girls and boys have two runs on the tumbling strip on which they are judged. The first is known as the straight run, in which the gymnast performs somersaults forward, backward and sideways. The second is known as the twisting run, in which the competitor shows his or her ability to incorporate twists into the somersaults. All tumbling is performed without the accompaniment of music. There are World Championship titles both for individual runs and for an overall title combining the scores of both.

The remaining sections of the sport—the pairs and group exercises—are performed on the ordinary gymnastics floor area. In each of the sections the gymnasts must complete two entirely different routines. The first is a balance exercise in which the gymnasts must show their ability to lift and balance their partners. The routine must include supports, pyramids and counterbalances. The second part is called the tempo routine, and the gymnasts must demonstrate agile dance movements as well as somersaults in the air.

Each of the exercises for pairs and groups is accompanied by music chosen by the gymnasts. The judges will deduct marks if they feel that the music is not suitable for the routine being performed. The time allowed for each section is between two and a half and three minutes.

Opposite Soviet sports acrobats Margarita Kuchorenko and Vassily Machuga in the mixed pairs event.

Right A one-handed balance is shown here by the Soviet women's pair, Margarita Kuchorenko and Nadejda Tischenko.

Above The Chinese acrobat team demonstrates a four-high balance.

16 Biographies and records of famous gymnasts

Nicolai Andrianov (born 1952, USSR)
1971 European Championships, Madrid

Individual Overall	Bronze
Floor	Bronze
Pommel Horse	Gold
Rings	Silver
Vault	Gold
Parallel Bars	Joint Silver

1972 Olympic Games, Munich

Team	Silver
Floor	Gold
Vault	Bronze

1973 European Championships, Grenoble

Individual Overall	Silver
Floor	Gold
Rings	Joint Silver
Vault	Gold
Parallel Bars	Joint Silver

1974 World Championships, Varna

Team	Silver
Individual Overall	Silver
Pommel Horse	Silver
Rings	Joint Gold
Vault	Silver
Parallel Bars	Silver

1975 European Championships, Berne

Individual Overall	Gold
Floor	Joint Gold
Pommel Horse	Silver
Vault	Gold
Parallel Bars	Gold
High Bar	Joint Gold

1975 World Cup, London

Individual Overall	Gold
Floor	Silver
Pommel Horse	Silver
Parallel Bars	Gold

1976 Olympic Games, Montreal

Team	Silver
Individual Overall	Gold
Floor	Gold
Pommel Horse	Bronze
Rings	Gold
Vault	Gold
Parallel Bars	Silver

1977 World Cup, Oviedo

Individual Overall	Joint Gold
Floor	Gold
Rings	Gold
Vault	Silver
Parallel Bars	Gold

1978 World Championships, Strasbourg

Team	Silver
Individual Overall	Gold
Rings	Gold
Vault	Silver
Parallel Bars	Silver

1979 World Championships, Fort Worth

Team	Gold
Vault	Silver

1980 Olympic Games, Moscow

Team	Gold
Individual Overall	Silver
Floor	Silver
Vault	Gold
High Bar	Bronze

Andrianov was nicknamed 'Old One Leg' by some coaches because of his extraordinary ability to keep his legs straight and together during extremely difficult exercises. He is also in charge of the Junior National Junior Boys Squad.

Vladimir Artemov (born 1964, USSR)
1982 Junior European Championships, Ankara

Individual Overall	Silver
Pommel Horse	Silver
Parallel Bars	Silver
Rings	Silver

1983 World Championships, Budapest

Team	Silver
Parallel Bars	Joint Gold

1985 World Championships, Montreal

Team	Gold
Individual Overall	Silver
Pommel Horse	4th
Vault	4th
Parallel Bars	4th
High Bar	5th

1986 World Cup, Beijing

Individual Overall	Bronze
Floor	7th
Pommel Horse	4th
Vault	5th

1987 World Championships, Rotterdam

Team	Gold
Individual Overall	Bronze
Floor	Silver
Parallel Bars	Gold
High Bar	Joint 5th

1988 USSR National Championships

Individual Overall	Joint Gold

1988 Olympic Games, Seoul

Team	Gold
Individual Overall	Gold
Floor	Silver
Parallel Bars	Gold
High Bar	Gold

Terry Bartlett (born 1963, Great Britain)
1983 World Championships, Budapest

Team	17th
Individual Overall	80th

1984 Olympic Games, Los Angeles

Team	9th
Individual Apparatus	36th

1985 European Championships, Oslo

Individual Overall	34th

Above Vladimir Artemov

1985 World Championships

Team	17th
Individual	73rd

1987 World Championships

Team	19th
Individual Overall	76th

1988 Olympic Games, Seoul

Individual Overall	75th

Above Terry Bartlett

Olga Bicherova (born 1966, USSR)
1981 European Championships, Madrid

Individual Overall	22nd
Vault	4th

1981 World Championships, Moscow

Team	Gold
Individual Overall	Gold

1982 World Cup, Zagreb
Individual Overall	Joint Gold
Vault	Joint Gold
Asymmetric Bars	Joint Silver
Beam	Bronze
Floor	Gold

1983 World Championships, Budapest
Team	Gold
Vault	5th

In the 1981 World Championships in Moscow, Olga was entered to give her a chance to learn from the much experienced Natalia Shaposhnikova. To everybody's surprise she not only performed well, but in front of a capacity audience of 18,000 she took the championships by storm and won the overall competition.

Dmetri Bilozerchev (born 1966, USSR)

1982 Junior European Championships, Ankara
Floor	Gold
Individual Overall	Gold
Pommel Horse	Gold
Rings	Gold
Parallel Bars	Gold
Vault	Gold
High Bar	Silver

1983 World Championships
Team	Silver
Individual Overall	Gold
Floor	Silver
Pommel Horse	Gold
Rings	Gold
Vault	6th
High Bar	Gold

1985 European Championships, Oslo
Individual Overall	Gold
Floor	Gold
Pommel Horse	Gold
Rings	Gold
Vault	Silver
Parallel Bars	Gold
High Bar	Joint Gold

1987 World Championships
Team	Gold
Individual Overall	Gold
Pommel Horse	Joint Gold
Rings	Joint Silver
Vault	Joint 4th
Parallel Bars	Silver
High Bar	Gold

1988 USSR National Championships
Individual Overall	Joint Gold

1988 Olympic Games, Seoul
Team	Gold
Individual Overall	Bronze
Pommel Horse	Joint Gold
Rings	Joint Gold

Svetlana Boginskaia (born 1973, USSR)

1986 Junior European Championships
Individual Overall	Gold
Vault	Silver
Asymmetric Bars	Silver
Beam	Gold

1987 World Championships
Team	Silver
Individual Beam	Joint Bronze

1988 Olympic Games, Seoul
Team	Gold
Individual Overall	Bronze
Vault	Gold
Asymmetric Bars	5th
Beam	5th
Floor	Silver

1988 USSR National Championships
Individual Overall	Silver

Vera Caslavska (born 1942, Czechoslovakia)

1959 European Championships, Cracovie
Vault	Silver
Beam	Gold

1963 European Championships, Leipzig
Individual Overall	Joint Bronze
Floor	Bronze

1962 World Championships, Prague
Team	Silver
Individual Overall	Silver
Vault	Gold
Floor	Bronze

1964 Olympic Games, Tokyo
Team	Silver
Individual Overall	Gold
Vault	Gold
Beam	Gold

1964 European Championships, Anvers
Individual Overall	Gold
Vault	Gold
Asymmetric Bars	Gold
Beam	Gold
Floor	Gold

1966 World Championships, Dortmund
Team	Gold
Individual Overall	Gold
Vault	Gold
Beam	Silver
Floor	Silver

1967 European Championships, Amsterdam
Individual Overall	Gold
Vault	Gold
Asymmetric Bars	Gold
Beam	Gold
Floor	Gold

1968 Olympic Games, Mexico
Team	Silver
Individual Overall	Gold
Vault	Gold
Asymmetric Bars	Gold
Beam	Silver
Floor	Joint Gold

Vera Caslavska is the only girl in the world to have won seven gold individual Olympic medals – three in 1964 and four in 1968. She now coaches gymnastics in Prague.

Nadia Comaneci (born 1961, Romania)

1975 European Championships, Skien
Individual Overall	Gold
Vault	Gold
Asymmetric Bars	Gold
Beam	Gold
Floor	Silver

1976 Olympic Games, Montreal
Team	Silver
Individual Overall	Gold
Asymmetric Bars	Gold
Beam	Gold
Floor	Bronze

1977 European Championships, Prague
Individual Overall	Gold
Vault	Silver
Asymmetric Bars	Joint Gold

1978 World Championships, Strasbourg
Team	Silver
Vault	Silver
Beam	Gold

1979 European Championships, Copenhagen
Individual Overall	Gold
Vault	Gold
Beam	Bronze
Floor	Gold

1979 World Championships, Fort Worth
Team	Gold

1980 Olympic Games, Moscow
Team	Silver
Individual Overall	Joint Silver
Beam	Gold
Floor	Joint Gold

Nadia Comaneci was the first girl in the world to score a full ten points in an Olympic Games. This she did seven times in 1976 in Montreal.

Bart Conner (born 1958, USA)

1976 Olympic Team

1976 American Cup
Individual Overall	Gold

1978 World Cup, Sao Paulo
Parallel Bars	Joint Silver

1979 World Championships, Fort Worth
Team	Bronze
Vault	Joint Bronze
Parallel Bars	Gold

1979 World Cup, Tokyo
Pommel Horse	Gold

1980 Final Olympic Trials
Individual Overall	Gold

1981 American Cup
Individual Overall	Gold

1981 World Championships, Moscow
Team	5th
Individual Overall	11th

1982 World Cup, Zagreb
Individual Overall	11th

1983 World Championships, Budapest
Team	4th
Individual Overall	11th
Floor	5th
Pommel Horse	7th
Parallel Bars	Joint 6th

1984 Olympic Games, Los Angeles
Team	Gold
Individual Overall	6th
Floor	5th
Parallel Bars	Gold

Conner is one of the greatest gymnasts ever produced by the United States.

Tim Daggett (born 1963, USA)

1981 World Championships,
Moscow
Team — 5th
Individual Overall — 70th

1984 Olympic Games,
Los Angeles
Team — Gold
Pommel Horse — Bronze
High Bar — Joint 4th

1984 USA National Championships,
Evanston
Individual Overall — 4th
Floor — 5th
Pommel Horse — Gold
Rings — Joint Silver
Parallel Bars — Joint Gold

1985 American Cup, Indianapolis
Individual Overall — Gold

1985 World Championships,
Montreal
Team — 9th
Individual Overall — 25th

1987 World Championships,
Rotterdam
Team — 9th
Individual Overall — 176th
(injured)

Kersten Dagmar (born 1970, East Germany)

1985 World Championships
Team — Bronze
Individual Overall — Bronze
Vault — Bronze
Asymmetric Bars — Silver
Beam — 8th
Floor — 6th

1988 Olympic Games, Seoul
Team — Bronze
Individual Overall — 8th
Vault — 6th
Asymmetric Bars — Silver

One of the latest young gymnasts to come from the DDR.

Natalie Davis (born 1966, Great Britain)

1983 Daily Mirror British
Championships, London
Individual Overall — 6th
Asymmetric Bars — Bronze
Beam — Silver
Floor — Gold

1984 Daily Mirror British
Championships, London
Individual Overall — Gold
Asymmetric Bars — Joint Silver
Beam — 6th
Floor — 6th

1984 Harrison Drape Champions
Cup, London
Individual Overall — Silver

1984 Olympic Games, Los
Angeles
Team — 7th
Individual Overall — 19th

Natalie Davis is now retired and coaching at one of Great Britain's leading clubs.

Alexander Detiatin (born 1957, USSR)

1975 European Championships,
Berne
Individual Overall — Bronze
Rings — Bronze
Parallel Bars — Silver

1975 World Cup, London
Individual Overall — Bronze

1976 Olympic Games, Montreal
Team — Silver
Rings — Silver

1978 World Championships,
Strasbourg
Team — Silver
Floor — Bronze
Rings — Silver

1978 World Cup, Sao Paulo
Individual Overall — Bronze
Floor — Bronze
Pommel Horse — Silver
Rings — Gold
Vault — Bronze
High Bar — Joint Bronze

1979 World Cup, Tokyo
Individual Overall — Gold
Rings — Gold
Vault — Silver
Parallel Bars — Silver
High Bar — Joint Silver

1979 European Championships,
Essen
Rings — Gold
Vault — Joint Gold
Parallel Bars — Silver

1979 World Championships,
Fort Worth
Team — Gold
Individual Overall — Gold
Rings — Gold
Vault — Gold
High Bar — Bronze

1980 Olympic Games, Moscow
Team — Gold
Individual Overall — Gold
Floor — Bronze
Pommel Horse — Silver
Rings — Gold
Vault — Silver
Parallel Bars — Silver
High Bar — Silver

1981 World Championships, Moscow
Team — Gold
Rings — Gold
Parallel Bars — Joint Gold

1982 World Cup, Zagreb
Individual Overall — 5th

Detiatin is the only man to have won medals in all eight categories, with three gold, four silver and one bronze at the 1980 Olympic Games in Moscow. He is now retired.

Aurelia Dobre (born 1972, Romania)

1986 Junior European
Championships
Individual Overall — Joint Bronze
Vault — Gold
Asymmetric Bars — Gold
Beam — Joint Silver

1987 World Championships,
Rotterdam
Team — Gold
Individual Overall — Gold
Vault — Bronze
Asymmetric Bars — Joint 4th
Beam — Silver
Floor — Silver

1988 Olympic Games, Seoul
Team — Silver
Individual Overall — 6th
Asymmetric Bars — 7th

Above Aurelia Dobre

Emilia Eberle (born 1964, Romania)

1978 European Junior
Championships, Milan
Individual Overall — Gold
Vault — Gold
Asymmetric Bars — Gold
Beam — Joint 4th
Floor — Joint Silver

1978 World Championships,
Strasbourg
Team — Silver
Individual Overall — 5th
Vault — 5th
Asymmetric Bars — Bronze
Beam — Bronze
Floor — Joint Bronze

1979 European Championships,
Copenhagen
Individual Overall — Silver
Vault — 7th
Asymmetric Bars — Silver
Beam — Silver
Floor — Joint 4th

1979 World Championships,
Fort Worth
Team — Gold
Individual Overall — 8th
Asymmetric Bars — Bronze
Floor — Gold

1979 World Cup, Tokyop
Individual Overall — Joint Silver
Vault — 8th
Asymmetric Bars — Joint Gold
Beam — Gold
Floor — Bronze

1980 Olympic Games, Moscow
Team Silver
Individual Overall 6th
Asymmetric Bars Silver
Beam 6th
Floor 5th

1980 World Cup, Toronto
Individual Overall Joint 8th
Beam 6th
Floor 4th

1981 European Championships, Madrid
Individual Overall 18th

1981 World Championships, Moscow
Team 4th

A much under-rated gymnast now retired to take up coaching. All her sporting career was played in the shadow of the great Nadia Comaneci, her team mate.

Lisa Elliott (born 1969, Great Britain)
1985 World Championships, Montreal
Team 16th
Individual Overall 88th

1986 British National Championships
Individual Overall Gold

1987 European Championships, Moscow
Individual Overall 24th

1987 British Championships
Individual Overall Gold

1987 World Championships, Rotterdam
Team 17th
Individual Overall 87th

1988 British Championships
Individual Overall Gold

Tong Fei (born 1961, China)
1981 World Championships, Moscow
Team Bronze
Individual Overall 4th
Rings 4th
Parallel Bars 6th
High Bar 8th

1982 World Cup, Zagreb
Individual Overall Silver
Floor Bronze
Pommel Horse 5th
Rings Bronze
Vault Bronze
Parallel Bars 5th
High Bar Joint Gold

1983 World Championships, Budapest
Team Gold
Individual Overall 35th
Floor Gold
Parallel Bars Bronze
High Bar Joint 4th

1984 Olympic Games, Los Angeles
Team Silver
Individual Overall 4th
Pommel Horse 4th
Rings 4th
Parallel Bars 4th
High Bar Silver

1985 World Championships, Montreal
Team Silver
Individual Overall 7th
Floor Gold
Parallel Bars 6th
High Bar Gold

Kelly Garrison-Stevens (born 1967, USA)
1983 World Championships, Budapest
Team 7th
Individual Overall 45th

1984 Pacific Alliance Silver
Games, Reno

1984 Pacific Alliance Gold
Games, San Francisco

1985 World Championships, Montreal
Team 6th
Individual Overall 18th

1985 Arthur Gander International
Overall position 5th

1987 World Championships, Rotterdam
Team Individual 76th
Overall

1988 Olympic Games, Seoul
Team 4th
Individual Overall 16th
Beam 7th

1988 USA Championships
Individual Overall Silver
Asymmetric Bars 5th
Beam Gold
Floor 6th

Mitch Gaylord (born 1961, USA)
1983 World Championships, Budapest
Team 4th
Individual Overall 8th

1984 USA National Championships, Evanston
Individual Overall Gold
Floor 4th
Pommel Horse Joint Bronze
Rings Gold
Vault Silver
Parallel Bars Bronze
High Bar 5th

1984 Olympic Games, Los Angeles
Team Gold
Individual Overall 5th
Rings Bronze
Vault Joint Silver
Parallel Bars Bronze

1984 American Cup, New York
Pommel Horse Joint Gold
Rings Gold

Now retired.

Eberhard Gienger (born 1951, Federal Republic of Germany)
1973 European Championships, Grenoble
High Bar Joint Gold

1974 World Championships, Varna
High Bar Gold

1975 European Championships, Berne
Individual Overall Silver
Pommel Horse Bronze
High Bar Joint Gold

1975 World Cup, London
High Bar Silver

1976 Olympic Games, Montreal
High Bar Bronze

1977 European Championships, Vilnius
Parallel Bars Joint Silver

1977 World Cup, Oviedo
High Bar Joint Gold

1978 World Championships, Strasbourg
Pommel Horse Silver
High Bar Silver

1981 World Championships, Moscow
Team 4th
Individual Overall 21st
High Bar Joint Silver

Gienger is perhaps the greatest ambassador of the sport. Apart from his native German, he speaks Russian, French and English. He is now a member of the Executive Committee of the World Governing Body of the International Federation of Gymnastics.

Maxi Gnauck (born 1964, DDR)
1979 World Championships, Forth Worth
Team Bronze
Individual Overall Silver
Vault 6th
Asymmetric Bars Joint Gold
Beam 6th
Floor 4th

1979 European Championships, Copenhagen
Individual Overall Joint 6th
Vault Silver
Asymmetric Bars Bronze

1981 European Championships, Madrid
Individual Overall Gold
Vault Joint Silver
Asymmetric Bars Gold
Beam Gold
Floor Gold

1981 World Championships, Moscow
Team Bronze
Vault Gold
Asymmetric Bars Gold
Beam Gold

1982 World Cup, Zagreb
Individual Overall 5th
Vault Joint 7th
Asymmetric Bars Gold
Floor Bronze

1983 World Championships, Budapest
Team Bronze
Individual Overall 7th
Vault 4th
Asymmetric Bars Gold
Beam 4th

103

Maxi was one of the most exciting and technically competent gymnasts ever produced in the DDR. She is now one of the country's leading coaches.

Koji Gushiken (born 1956, Japan)

1979 World Championships,
Fort Worth
Team	Silver
Individual Overall	7th
Pommel Horse	Bronze
Rings	4th
Parallel Bars	Joint 4th

1980 World Cup, Toronto
Individual Overall	Bronze
Floor	8th
Pommel Horse	Joint Silver
Rings	Joint Bronze
Parallel Bars	Joint 6th
High Bar	Joint Gold

1981 World Championships, Moscow
Team	Silver
Individual Overall	Bronze
Floor	Bronze
Pommel Horse	7th
Parallel Bars	Joint Gold
High Bar	6th

1982 World Cup, Zagreb
Individual Overall	Joint 8th
Rings	Joint 5th
Pommel Horse	Silver
Parallel Bars	Silver

1983 World Championships,
Budapest
Team	Bronze
Individual Overall	Silver
Pommel Horse	8th
Rings	Joint Gold
Parallel Bars	5th

1984 Olympic Games, Los
Angeles
Team	Bronze
Individual Overall	Gold
Floor	8th
Rings	Gold
Vault	Joint Silver
Parallel Bars	5th
High Bar	Bronze

1985 World Championships,
Montreal
Team	4th
Individual Overall	13th
Parallel Bars	Bronze

Retired in 1986 to take up a coach position with the National Federation.

Karen Hargate (born 1972, Great Britain)

1987 European Championships,
Moscow
Individual Overall	27th

1987 World Championships,
Rotterdam
Team	17th
Individual Overall	90th

1988 Olympic Games, Seoul
Individual Overall	82nd

A rising star of British gymnastics.

James Hartung born 1960, USA)

1975 USA National Junior
Championships
Individual Overall	Gold

1976 Junior Olympic National
Champion

1977 Junior Olympic National
Champion

1978 World Championships,
Strasbourg
Team	4th

1978 USA National Championships
Individual Overall	Bronze

1979 World Championships,
Fort Worth
Team	Bronze
Individual Overall	Joint 9th
Vault	8th

1980 World Cup, Toronto
Individual Overall	11th

1981 American Cup
Individual Overall	Silver

1981 USA Championships
Individual Overall	Gold

1981 World Championships, Moscow
Team	5th
Individual Overall	15th

1982 World Cup, Zagreb
Individual Overall	10th
Floor	6th
Vault	Joint 5th
Parallel Bars	7th

1984 Olympic Games, Los
Angeles
Team	Gold
Vault	6th

Following in the famous steps of Thomas and Conner was no easy task, but Hartung as a gymnast was every bit as good as his two star team-mates.

Karin Janz (born 1952, DDR)

1967 European Championships,
Amsterdam
Individual Overall	4th
Vault	Bronze
Asymmetric Bars	Silver
Beam	4th

1968 Olympic Games, Mexico
Team	Bronze
Asymmetric Bars	Silver
Beam	4th

1969 European Championships,
Landskrona
Individual Overall	Gold
Vault	Gold
Asymmetric Bars	Gold
Beam	Gold
Floor	Silver

1970 World Championships,
Ljubljana
Team	Silver
Vault	Silver
Asymmetric Bars	Gold

1972 Olympic Games, Munich
Team	Silver
Individual Overall	Silver
Vault	Gold
Asymmetric Bars	Gold
Beam	Bronze

One of the most colourful gymnasts of the women gymnastics stars of the 1960s. She competed in the era when such stars as Caslavska, Tourischeva and Latynina were still at their best or reaching their best.

Brandy Johnson (born 1973, USA)

1988 Olympic Games, Seoul
Team	4th
Individual Overall	10th
Vault	5th

1988 USA Championships
Individual Overall	Joint 6th
Vault	Joint Bronze
Beam	5th
Floor	Silver

Kathy Johnson (born 1959, USA)

1978 America Cup, New York
Individual Overall	Gold

1978 World Championships,
Strasbourg
Team	5th
Individual overall	8th
Floor	Bronze

1978 USA National Championships,
New York
Individual Overall	Gold
Beam	Gold
Floor	Gold

1978 World Cup, Sao Paulo
Floor	Bronze

1979 USA National Championships,
Dayton
Individual Overall	4th
Beam	Silver

1979 World Cup, Tokyo
Individual Overall	6th

1979 World Championships,
Fort Worth
Team	6th

1981 Daily Mirror Champions All,
London
Individual Overall	Silver

1981 USA National Championships,
Bethlehem, Pa.
Individual Overall	Silver
Beam	Bronze
Floor	Silver

1981 World Championships, Moscow
Team	6th

1983 World Championships,
Budapest
Team	7th
Individual Overall	11th
Floor	8th

1983 USA National Championships,
Chicago
Individual Overall	5th
Vault	6th
Asymmetric Bars	Joint 5th
Beam	Silver
Floor	4th

1984 USA National Championships,
Evanston
Individual Overall	6th
Vault	4th
Beam	Joint Bronze
Floor	7th

1984 Olympic Games, Los
 Angeles
 Team   Silver
 Individual Overall   10th
 Beam   Bronze

One of the most consistent world-class gymnasts ever produced by the USA. Retired in 1985.

Above Scott Johnson

Scott Johnson (born 1961, USA)
1983 World Championships,
 Budapest
 Team   4th

1984 USA National Championships,
 Evanston
 Individual Overall   5th
 Pommel Horse   7th
 Rings   6th
 Vault   Bronze
 Parallel Bars   4th

1984 Olympic Games, Los
 Angeles
 Team   Gold
 Individual Overall   Gold

1985 World Championships,
 Montreal
 Team   9th
 Individual Overall   22nd

1987 World Championships,
 Rotterdam
 Team   9th
 Individual Overall   167th

1987 USA Championships
 Individual Overall   Gold

1988 Olympic Games, Seoul
 Team   11th
 Individual Overall   63rd

Scott Johnson has been one of the regular members of the USA team throughout the eighties.

Hiroji Kajiyama (born 1953, Japan)
1974 World Championships, Varna
 Team   Gold
 Individual Overall   4th
 Floor   Silver
 Vault   Bronze
 Parallel Bars   4th

1975 World Cup, London
 Individual Overall   Silver
 Floor   Gold
 Pommel Horse   Bronze
 Vault   Silver
 Parallel Bars   Joint Silver
 High Bar   Bronze

1976 Olympic Games, Montreal
 Team   Gold
 Individual Overall   5th
 Vault   Bronze

1977 World Cup, Oviedo
 Individual Overall   7th
 Pommel Horse   5th
 Rings   4th
 Vault   Joint 4th

1978 World Championships,
 Strasbourg
 Team   Gold
 Individual Overall   5th
 Parallel Bars   Joint Silver

1979 World Championships,
 Fort Worth
 Team   Silver
 Individual Overall   Joint 9th
 Parallel Bars   6th
 High Bars   7th

1979 World Cup, Tokyo
 Individual Overall   9th
 Floor   Bronze
 Rings   Joint Bronze
 High Bar   Joint Silver

1980 World Cup, Toronto
 Individual Overall   8th
 Vault   Joint Silver

Nicknamed the 'Grasshopper' by his team mates for his incredible performances on the floor. Now retired to take up teaching. Considered one of the best all-round gymnasts of his time.

Eizo Kenmotsu (born 1948, Japan)
1968 Olympic Games, Mexico
 Team   Gold
 Individual Overall   4th
 Floor   6th
 Pommel Horse   5th
 Vault   6th
 Parallel Bars   5th
 High Bar   Bronze

1970 World Championships,
 Ljublijana
 Team   Gold
 Individual Overall   Gold
 Floor   Silver
 Pommel Horse   Silver
 Rings   4th
 Vault   5th
 Parallel   Joint Silver
 High Bars   Gold

1972 Olympic Games, Munich
 Team   Gold
 Individual Overall   Silver
 Floor   4th
 Pommel Horse   Bronze
 Rings   5th
 Vault   Joint 4th
 Parallel Bar   Bronze
 High Bar   4th

1974 World Championships, Varna
 Team   Gold
 Individual Overall   Bronze
 Pommel Horse   Bronze
 Vault   5th
 Parallel Bars   Gold
 High Bar   Joint Bronze

1976 Olympic Games, Montreal
 Team   Gold
 Floor   6th
 Pommel Horse   Silver
 Rings   5th
 High Bar   Silver

1978 World Championships,
 Strasbourg
 Team   Gold
 Individual Overall   Silver
 Rings   6th
 Vault   8th
 Parallel Bars   Gold
 High Bar   8th

1978 World Cup, Sao Paulo
 Individual Overall   4th
 Pommel Horse   Joint 5th
 Rings   7th
 Parallel Bars   5th
 High Bar   7th

1979 World Championships, Fort Worth
 Team   Silver

1979 World Cup, Tokyo
 Individual Overall   5th
 Parallel Bars   Gold
 High Bar   Joint Silver

He became a legend in his own lifetime. Known throughout the gymnastics world as the toughest gymnast ever produced by the Asian countries. His record of medals is unlikely to be matched by a fellow countryman in the foreseeable future.

Nelli Kim (born 1957, USSR)
1974 World Championships, Varna
 Team   Gold
 Beam   Bronze

1975 European Championships, Skien
 Individual Overall   Silver
 Vault   Joint Bronze
 Asymmetric Bars   Bronze
 Beam   Silver
 Floor   Gold

1976 Olympic Games, Montreal
 Team   Gold
 Individual Overall   Silver
 Vault   Gold
 Floor   Gold

1977 European Championships, Prague
 Individual Overall   Bronze
 Vault   Gold
 Beam   Silver
 Floor   Bronze

1978 World Championships, Strasbourg
 Team   Gold
 Vault   Gold
 Floor   Joint Gold

1979 World Championships, Fort Worth
 Team   Silver
 Individual Overall   Gold
 Vault   Joint Bronze
 Beam   Silver
 Floor   Silver

1979 World Cup, Tokyo
Individual Overall   Joint Silver
Vault   Bronze
Beam   Bronze
Floor   8th

1980 Olympic Games, Moscow
Team   Gold
Floor   Gold

Nelli Kim was one of the all-time greats of Soviet gymnasts. She was the second girl in the world to score a full 10 marks at the Olympic Games. She is now retired and has become a coach. She is also a leading World Governing Body (FIG) judge and as such travels the world officiating at events.

Olga Korbut (born 1955, USSR)
1972 Olympic Games, Munich
Team   Gold
Asymmetric Bars   Silver
Beam   Gold
Floor   Gold

1973 World Championships, London
Individual Overall   Silver

1974 World Championships, Varna
Team   Gold
Individual Overall   Silver
Vault   Gold
Asymmetric Bars   Silver
Beam   Silver
Floor   Silver

1975 World Cup, London
Individual Overall   Silver

1976 Olympic Games, Montreal
Team   Gold
Beam   Silver

Olga Korbut was the first girl in the world to perform a somersault on the beam. This she did during the 1972 Olympic Games. She arrived as a little-known competitor. By the time she had left the Games, Olga had become world famous.

Yuri Korolev (born 1962, USSR)
1981 Hunt International, London
Team   Gold
Individual Overall   Gold

1981 Moscow New International, Moscow
Individual Overall   Gold

1981 USSR Championships
Individual Overall   8th
Floor   Gold

1981 World Championships, Moscow
Team   Gold
Individual Overall   Gold
Floor   Gold
Parallel bars   Joint Bronze

1981 European Championships, Rome
Individual Overall   Silver
Floor   Gold
Pommel Horse   Joint Silver
Rings   Gold
Vault   Silver

1982 World Cup, Zagreb
Individual Overall   Bronze
Floor   Silver
Pommel Horse   Silver
Rings   Silver
Vault   Joint Bronze
Parallel Bars   Gold

1983 World Championships, Budapest
Team   Silver
Floor   4th

1983 European Championships, Varna
Individual Overall   Silver
Floor   Joint Gold
Pommel Horse   Joint Silver
Vault   Bronze
Parallel Bars   Gold

1985 World Championships, Montreal
Team   Gold
Individual Overall   Gold
Floor   Gold
Rings   Joint Gold
Pommel Horse   Gold

1986 World Cup, Beijing
Individual Overall   Gold
Floor   Silver
Rings   Joint Gold
Vault   Joint Gold
Parallel Bars   Bronze
High Bar   Gold

1987 European Championships, Moscow
Individual Overall   Silver
Floor   Silver
Pommel Horse   5th
Vault   Gold

1987 World Championships, Rotterdam
Team   Gold
Individual Overall   Silver
Pommel Horse   4th
Rings   Gold
Vault   Joint 4th

Never has a male gymnast caused a greater sensation in gymnastics than when this young man exploded on to the scene in the European Championships and World Championships of 1981. History will remember him as one of the great Soviet gymnasts.

Sylvio Kroll (born 1965, East Germany)
1983 World Championships, Budapest
Team   5th
Individual Overall   15th
Floor   7th
Pommel Horse   5th
Vault   4th

1985 European Championships, Oslo
Individual Overall   4th
Pommel Horse   Joint Silver
Vault   Gold
Parallel Bars   Silver
High Bars   5th

1985 World Championships, Montreal
Team   Bronze
Individual Overall   Bronze
Floor   4th
Pommel Horse   6th
Rings   8th
Vault   7th
Parallel Bars   Joint Gold
High Bar   Silver

1986 World Cup, Beijing
Individual Overall   4th
Floor   Bronze
Pommel Horse   8th
Vault   Joint Gold
Parallel Bars   5th
High Bar   Silver

Above Sylvio Kroll

1987 World Championships, Rotterdam
Team   Bronze
Individual Overall   4th
Pommel Horse   5th
Vault   Joint Gold
Parallel Bars   4th

1988 Olympic Games, Seoul
Team   Silver
Individual Overall   Joint 10th
Pommel Horse   8th
Vault   Silver
Parallel Bars   7th

Charles Lakes (born 1964, USA)
1985 World Championships, Montreal
Team   9th
Individual Overall   58th

1987 World Championships, Rotterdam
Team   9th
Individual Overall   51st

1988 Olympic Games, Seoul
Team   11th
Individual Overall   19th

1988 USA Championships
Individual Overall   Bronze
Floor   Joint Gold
Parallel Bars   6th

Natalia Laschenova (born 1974, USSR)
1986 Belgium Masters International, Brussels
Individual Overall   Gold

1988 1st European Cup, Florence
Individual Overall   Bronze
Asymmetric Bars   Gold
Beam   Bronze

1988 USSR National Championships
Individual Overall   Bronze

1988 Olympic Games, Seoul
Team   Gold
Individual Overall   5th

Larissa Latynina (born 1934, USSR)
1956 Olympic Games, Melbourne
Team	Gold
Individual Overall	Gold
Vault	Gold
Floor	Joint Gold

1957 European Championships, Bucharest
Individual Overall	Gold
Vault	Gold
Asymmetric Bars	Gold
Beam	Gold
Floor	Gold

1958 World Championships, Moscow
Team	Gold
Individual Overall	Gold
Vault	Gold
Asymmetric Bars	Gold
Beam	Gold
Floor	Silver

1960 Olympic Games, Rome
Team	Gold
Individual Overall	Gold
Vault	Bronze
Asymmetric Bars	Silver
Beam	Silver
Floor	Gold

1961 European Championships, Leipzig
Individual Overall	Gold
Asymmetric Bars	Silver
Beam	Silver
Floor	Gold

1962 World Championships, Prague
Team	Gold
Individual Overall	Gold
Vault	Silver
Asymmetric Bars	Bronze
Beam	Silver
Floor	Gold

1964 Olympic Games, Tokyo
Team	Gold
Individual Overall	Silver
Vault	Silver
Beam	Bronze
Floor	Gold

1965 European Championships, Sofia
Individual Overall	Silver
Vault	Bronze
Asymmetric Bars	Silver
Beam	Silver
Floor	Joint Silver

Larissa is the only girl to have ever won fifteen World gold medals – ten individual and five team. She also won nine Olympic gold medals (six individual and three team) and a total of five silver and four bronze medals at Olympic level.

Valeri Liukin (born 1966, USSR)
1985 USSR National
Junior	Silver

1986 National Youth Champion

1987 World Championships
Team	Gold

1987 European Overall Champion
European Floor Champion
European Pommel Horse Champion
European Parallel Bars Champion
European High Bar Champion

1988 USSR National Championship
Individual Overall	Joint Silver

1988 Olympic Games, Seoul
Team	Gold
Individual Overall	Silver
Parallel Bars	Silver
High Bar	Silver

The only gymnast in the world to perform a triple back somersault in a floor exercise. Although gymnastics is his first love, he is also an accomplished speed skater.

Zoltan Magyar (born 1953, Hungary)
1972 Olympic Games, Munich
Team	9th
Individual Overall	Joint 29th

1973 European Championships, Grenoble
Individual Overall	Joint 17th
Pommel Horse	Gold

1974 World Championships, Varna
Team	4th
Individual Overall	15th
Pommel Horse	Gold

1975 World Cup, London
Individual Overall	7th
Floor	6th
Pommel Horse	Gold

1975 European Championships, Berne
Individual Overall	4th
Pommel Horse	Gold
Vault	4th
Parallel Bars	4th

1976 Olympic Games, Montreal
Team	4th
Individual Overall	9th
Pommel Horse	Gold
Vault	Joint 5th

Above Valeri Liukin

1977 European Championships, Vilnius
Individual Overall	8th
Pommel Horse	Gold
Vault	4th
Parallel Bars	5th
High Bar	Joint 5th

1978 World Cup, Sao Paulo
Individual Overall	5th
Pommel Horse	Gold
Parallel Bars	5th
High Bar	8th

1978 World Championships, Strasbourg
Team	6th
Individual Overall	12th
Pommel Horse	Gold

1979 World Championships, Fort Worth
Team	6th
Individual Overall	18th
Pommel Horse	Gold

1980 Olympic Games, Moscow
Team	Bronze
Individual Overall	Joint 9th
Pommel Horse	Gold

Magyar led the way to the full ten mark for men gymnasts with his incredibly consistent performance on the pommel horse.

Julianne McNamara (born 1965, USA)
1980 USA National Championships, Utah
Individual Overall	Gold

1981 USA National Championships, Bethlehem, Pa.
Individual Overall	4th
Asymmetric Bars	Gold

1981 America Cup, Fort Worth
Individual Overall	Gold

1981 World Championships, Moscow
Team	6th
Individual Overall	Joint 7th
Asymmetric Bars	Joint Bronze
Beam	5th
Floor	7th

1982 USA National Championships, Salt Lake City
Individual Overall	Silver

1982 America Cup, New York
Individual Overall	Joint Gold

1982 Australa Cup, Melbourne
Individual Overall	Gold
Vault	Gold
Asymmetric Bars	Gold
Beam	Gold
Floor	Gold

1982 World Cup, Zagreb
Individual Overall	8th
Vault	Bronze
Beam	7th

1983 America Cup, New York
Individual Overall	Silver
Asymmetric Bars	Joint Gold

1983 World Championships, Budapest
Team	7th
Individual Overall	16th
Vault	Joint 6th
Asymmetric Bars	7th

1983 USA National Championships,
Chicago
Individual Overall   Silver
Vault   4th
Asymmetric Bars   Gold
Floor   7th

1984 America Cup, New York
Individual Overall   Bronze

1984 USA National Championships,
Evanston
Individual Overall   Silver
Vault   5th
Asymmetric Bars   Gold
Beam   Joint Bronze
Floor   Joint Silver

1984 Olympic Games, Los Angeles
Team   Silver
Individual Overall   4th
Asymmetric Bars   Joint Gold
Floor   Silver

Retired in 1985 to take up coaching.

Phoebe Mills (born 1972, USA)
1985 International Europe, Avignon
Individual Overall   Bronze

1987 World Championships,
Rotterdam
Team   6th
Individual Overall   48th

1988 Olympic Games, Seoul
Team   4th
Individual Overall   15th
Asymmetric Bars   8th
Beam   Joint Bronze
Floor   6th

1988 USA Championships
Individual Overall   Gold
Asymmetric Bars   4th
Beam   Bronze
Floor   Gold

Holds international age group Speed
Skating Record for 500 metres.

Valentine Mogilny (born 1965, USSR)
1985 Moscow International
Individual Overall   Bronze

1985 World Championships, Montreal
Team   Gold
Individual Overall   6th
Floor   6th
Pommel Horse   Gold
Parallel Bars   Joint Gold

1985 European Championships, Oslo
Individual Overall   Silver
Floor   4th
Pommel Horse   4th
Rings   Silver
Vault   8th
High Bar   8th

1986 World Cup, Beijing
Individual Overall   Joint 4th
Pommel Horse   Silver
Rings   Joint Gold
Parallel Bars   Joint Gold
High Bar   6th

1987 European Championships,
Moscow
Individual Overall   5th
Rings   Gold
Parallel Bars   7th
High Bar   8th

1988 Olympic Games, Seoul. Selected
and attended, but became injured
and had to withdraw.

1988 USSR National Championships
Individual Overall   4th

His coach believes his best is yet to
come.

Andrew Morris (born 1961, Great
Britain)
1981 World Championships, Moscow
Team   17th
Individual Overall   Joint 96th

1983 World Championships,
Budapest
Team   17th
Individual Overall   67th

1983 Daily Mirror British
Championships, London
Individual Overall   Gold
Floor   5th
Pommel Horse   Gold
Rings   Silver
Vault   Bronze

1983 British National
Championships, London
Individual Overall   Gold

1983 European Championships, Varna
Individual Overall   14th

1983 World Championships,
Budapest
Team   17th
Individual Overall   67th

1984 Olympic Games, Los Angeles
Team   9th
Individual Overall   24th

1984 British National
Championships, London
Individual Overall   Gold

1985 European Championships, Oslo
Individual Overall   Joint 14th

1986 British National
Championships, London
Individual Overall   Gold

1987 European Championships,
Moscow
Individual Overall   21st

1987 British National
Championships, London
Individual Overall   Gold

1987 World Championships,
Rotterdam
Team   19th
Individual Overall   75th

1988 Olympic Games, Seoul
Team   19th
Individual Overall   81st

Li Ning (born 1963, People's Republic
of China)
1982 World Cup, Zagreb
Individual Overall   Gold
Floor   Gold
Pommel Horse   Gold
Rings   Gold
Vault   Gold
Parallel Bars   Bronze
High Bar   Joint Gold

1983 World Championships, Budapest
Team   Gold
Individual Overall   6th
Floor   Bronze
Pommel Horse   4th
Rings   Bronze
Vault   Silver

1984 Olympic Games, Los Angeles
Team   Silver
Individual Overall   Bronze
Floor   Gold
Pommel Horse   Gold
Rings   Silver
Vault   Silver
Parallel Bars   6th

1986 World Cup, Beijing
Individual Overall   Joint Gold
Floor   Gold
Pommel Horse   Gold
Rings   Bronze
High Bar   8th

1987 World Championships, Rotterdam
Team   Silver
Individual overall   174th
Pommel Horse   7th
Rings   Joint Silver

1988 Olympic Games, Seoul
Team   4th
Individual Overall   50th
Floor   5th

Above Oksana Omelianchik

Oksana Omelianchik (born 1970,
USSR)
1985 European Championships,
Helsinki
Individual Overall   Bronze
Vault   5th
Asymmetric Bars   Bronze
Beam   Gold
Floor   Silver

1986 World Cup, Beijing
Individual Overall   Bronze
Vault   Silver
Asymmetric Bars   Silver
Beam   Gold
Floor   Bronze

1987 World Championships, Rotterdam
Team   Silver
Individual Overall   5th

1988 USSR National Championships,
Moscow
Individual Overall   8th

1988 Olympic Games, Seoul
Selected for team and attended.
Injury prevented participation.

Hayley Price (born 1966, Great Britain)
1981 World Championships,
Moscow
Team   12th
Individual Overall   71st

1983 World Championships, Budapest
Team   17th
Individual Overall   82nd

1983 Daily Mirror British
Championships, London
Individual Overall   Gold
Asymmetric Bars   Gold
Beam   4th
Floor   Joint 5th

1983 Coca-Cola International,
London
Individual Overall   7th
Vault   Silver
Floor   6th

1984 Daily Mirror British
Championships, London
Individual Overall   Bronze
Vault   Bronze
Asymmetric Bars   6th
Beam   Silver
Floor   4th

1984 Harrison Drape
Champions Cup, London
Individual Overall   4th

1984 Olympic Games, Los Angeles
Team   7th
Individual Overall   43rd

1985 European Championships,
Helsinki
Individual Overall   31st

1985 World Championships,
Montreal
Team   16th
Individual Overall   112th

Hayley Price was the only British
woman gymnast to have a vault named
after her. This was a vault she
perfected at Wembley during a major
international which won her a gold
medal.

Mary Lou Retton (born 1968, USA)
1983 America Cup, New York
Individual Overall   Gold
Vault   Gold
Asymmetric Bars   Joint Gold
Floor   Gold

1983 South African Cup,
Cape Town
Individual Overall   Gold
Vault   Gold
Asymmetric Bars   Gold
Beam   Gold
Floor   Gold

1983 Chunichi Cup, Nagoya
Individual Overall   Gold
Vault   Gold

1983 USA National Championships,
Chicago
Individual Overall   Joint Bronze
Vault   Silver
Asymmetric Bars   Joint Silver
Beam   8th
Floor   5th

1984 America Cup, New York
Individual Overall   Gold

1984 USA National Championships,
Evanston
Individual Overall   Gold
Vault   Gold
Asymmetric Bars   4th
Beam   Joint Bronze
Floor   Gold

1984 Olympic Games, Los Angeles
Team   Silver
Individual Overall   Gold
Vault   Silver
Asymmetric Bars   Bronze
Beam   4th
Floor   Bronze

Mary Lou became the first USA
gymnast to capture the Olympic
women's title. After her success at the
Olympic Games in 1984 she retired to
become a television commentator.

Boris Schakhlin (born 1932, USSR)
1956 Olympic Games, Melbourne
Team   Gold
Pommel Horse   Gold

1958 World Championships, Moscow
Team   Gold
Individual Overall   Gold
Pommel Horse   Gold
Parallel Bars   Gold
High Bar   Gold

1960 Olympic Games, Rome
Team   Silver
Individual Overall   Gold
Pommel Horse   Joint Gold
Rings   Silver
Vault   Joint Gold
Parallel Bars   Gold
High Bar   Bronze

1962 World Championships, Prague
Team   Silver
Individual Overall   Bronze
Pommel Horse   Silver
Rings   Joint Silver
Vault   Joint Bronze
Parallel Bars   Silver

1963 European Championships,
Belgrade
Individual Overall   Silver
Pommel Horse   Bronze
Rings   Joint Gold
Parallel Bars   Silver
High Bar   Joint Gold

1964 Olympic Games, Tokyo
Team   Silver
Individual Overall   Joint Silver
Rings   Bronze
High Bar   Gold

Schakhlin is known as 'The Iron Man'
of gymnastics who bathes in cold
water even in winter in Russia! He is
now a much-respected judge at world-
class competitions.

Elfi Schlegel (born 1964, Canada)
1977 Canadian National
Championships
Individual Overall   Silver

1978 Canadian National
Championships
Individual Overall   Gold

1978 World Championships,
Strasbourg
Team   8th
Individual Overall   22nd

1978 Commonwealth Games,
Edmonton, Canada
Team   Gold
Individual Overall   Gold

1979 World Championships,
Fort Worth
Team   10th
Individual Overall   Joint 20th

1979 Canadian National
Championships
Individual Overall   Silver

1980 World Cup, Toronto
Vault   Joint Bronze

1981 Ennia Gold Cup, Holland
Individual Overall   5th
Beam   Joint Silver

1981 World Championships, Moscow
Team   10th

1983 World Championships,
Budapest
Team   10th
Individual Overall   70th

One of the most successful women
gymnasts ever produced by Canada.

Above Elena Shoushounova

Elena Shoushounova (born 1969,
USSR)
1982 Junior European
Championships, Ankara
Individual Overall   15th
Floor   Joint Gold

1986 World Cup

Individual Overall	Gold
Vault	Gold
Asymmetric Bars	Gold
Beam	Bronze
Floor	Gold

1987 European Championships

Individual Overall	Joint Bronze
Vault	Gold
Beam	4th
Floor	7th

1987 World Championships

Team	Silver
Individual Overall	Silver
Vault	Gold
Asymmetric Bars	Bronze
Beam	Silver
Floor	Joint Gold

1988 Olympic Games, Seoul

Team	Gold
Individual Overall	Gold
Vault	8th
Asymmetric Bars	Bronze
Beam	Silver
Floor	7th

1988 USSR Championships

Individual Overall	Gold

Daniela Silivas (born 1970, Romania)

1985 World Championships, Montreal

Team	Silver
Individual Overall	7th
Beam	Gold
Floor	Joint 4th

1986 World Cup, Beijing

Individual Overall	Silver
Vault	4th
Asymmetric Bars	Bronze
Beam	Silver
Floor	4th

1987 European Championships, Moscow

Individual Overall	Gold
Vault	Silver
Asymmetric Bars	Gold
Beam	Gold
Floor	Gold

1987 World Championships, Moscow

Team	Gold
Individual Overall	Bronze
Floor	Joint Gold

1988 Olympic Games, Seoul

Team	Silver
Individual Overall	Silver
Vault	Bronze
Asymmetric Bars	Gold
Beam	Gold
Floor	Gold

Boriana Stoyanova (born 1968, Bulgaria)

1982 Junior European Championships

Individual Overall	Silver
Vault	Joint Silver
Asymmetric Bars	Joint 4th
Beam	8th
Floor	4th

1983 World Championships, Budapest

Team	4th
Individual Overall	4th
Vault	Gold
Floor	Bronze

1985 World Championships, Montreal

Team	4th
Individual Overall	11th
Vault	5th

1986 World Cup, Beijing

Individual Overall	6th
Vault	6th
Asymmetric Bars	8th
Beam	6th
Floor	5th

1987 European Championships, Moscow

Individual Overall	6th
Vault	8th
Asymmetric Bars	6th
Floor	4th

1987 World Championships, Rotterdam

Team	5th
Individual Overall	10th
Vault	5th

Above Daniela Silivas

1988 1st European Cup, Florence

Individual Overall	Silver
Vault	Gold
Asymmetric Bars	4th
Beam	Silver
Floor	Silver

1988 Olympic Games, Seoul

Team	5th
Individual Overall	13th
Vault	4th

Ecaterina Szabo (born 1967, Romania)

1983 European Championships, Goteborg

Individual Overall	Joint Bronze
Vault	Silver
Asymmetric Bars	Gold
Floor	Joint Gold

1983 World Championships, Budapest

Team	Silver
Individual Overall	4th
Vault	Joint Silver
Asymmetric Bars	Joint Silver
Floor	Gold

1984 Olympic Games, Los Angeles

Team	Gold
Individual Overall	Silver
Vault	Gold
Beam	Silver
Floor	Gold

1985 World Championships, Montreal

Team	Silver
Individual Overall	5th
Vault	Silver
Asymmetric Bars	6th
Beam	Silver
Floor	4th

1985 European Championships, Helsinki

Individual Overall	5th
Vault	Silver
Beam	6th
Floor	6th

1986 World Cup, Beijing

Individual Overall	4th
Vault	Bronze
Asymmetric Bars	5th
Beam	4th

1987 World Championships, Rotterdam

Team	Gold
Individual Overall	14th
Beam	Bronze

1987 European Champion, Moscow

1988 Olympic Games, Seoul
Did not attend.

One of the many world stars produced by the Romanian system.

Tracee Talavera (born 1966, USA)

1980 USA National Championships, Utah

Individual Overall	Silver

1980 America Cup, New York

Individual Overall	Gold

1981 USA National Championships, Bethlehem, Pa.

Individual Overall	Gold

1981 World Championships, Moscow

Team	6th
Individual Overall	20th
Beam	Bronze

1981 America Cup, Fort Worth

Individual Overall	Silver

1982 America Cup, New York

Individual Overall	Silver

1982 USA National Championships, Salt Lake City

Individual Overall	Gold
Vault	5th
Asymmetric Bars	Silver
Beam	Silver
Floor	4th

1984 USA National Championships, Evanston
Individual Overall	8th
Vault	Bronze
Beam	Joint Gold
Floor	Joint 5th

1984 Olympic Games, Los Angeles
Team	Silver
Individual Overall	16th
Vault	4th

A very talented gymnast throughout her career. Always among the top four from 1980-1984. Now retired.

Kurt Thomas (born 1956, USA)
1976 Olympic Games, Montreal
Team	7th
Individual Overall	21st

1978 World Championships, Strasbourg
Floor	Gold

1979 World Championships, Fort Worth
Team	Bronze
Individual Overall	Silver
Floor	Joint Gold
Pommel Horse	Silver
Parallel Bar	Joint Silver
High Bar	Gold

1979 World Cup, Tokyo
Individual Overall	4th
Floor	6th
Pommel Horse	Bronze
Parallel Bars	8th
High Bar	5th

Kurt introduced the 'windmill' into the floor exercise. This aspect of floor work is now part of all leading world gymnastics.

Yuri Titov (born 1935, USSR)
1956 Olympic Games, Melbourne
Team	Gold
Individual Overall	Bronze
High Bar	Silver

1975 European Championships, Paris
Individual Overall	Silver
Rings	Silver
Vault	Gold
High Bar	Bronze

1958 World Championships, Moscow
Team	Gold
Individual Overall	Bronze
Floor	Bronze
Rings	Bronze
Vault	Gold
High Bar	Joint Bronze

1959 European Championships, Copenhagen
Individual Overall	Gold
Floor	Bronze
Pommel Horse	Gold
Rings	Gold
Vault	Joint Gold
Parallel Bars	Gold
High Bar	Silver

1960 Olympic Games, Rome
Team	Silver
Individual Overall	Bronze
Floor	Silver

1961 European Championships, Luxembourg
Individual Overall	Bronze
Rings	Joint Gold
High Bar	Gold

1962 World Championships, Prague
Team	Silver
Individual Overall	Gold
Rings	Gold

1964 Olympic Games, Tokyo
Team	Silver
High Bar	Silver

Titov has been one of the most outstanding male gymnasts of all time. He is President of the World Governing Body of the sport, the FIG.

Ludmila Tourischeva (born 1952, USSR)
1968 Olympic Games, Mexico
Team	Gold

1968 European Championships, Landskrona
Individual Overall	Joint Bronze
Asymmetric Bars	Bronze
Floor	Joint Bronze

1970 World Championships, Ljubljana
Team	Gold
Individual Overall	Gold
Vault	Joint Bronze
Asymmetric Bars	Silver
Floor	Gold

1971 European Championships, Madrid
Individual Overall	Joint Gold
Vault	Gold
Asymmetric Bars	Silver
Beam	Silver
Floor	Gold

1972 Olympic Games, Munich
Team	Gold
Individual Overall	Gold
Vault	Bronze
Floor	Silver

1972 European Championships, London
Individual Overall	Gold
Vault	Joint Gold
Asymmetric Bars	Gold
Beam	Gold
Floor	Gold

1974 World Championships, Varna
Team	Gold
Individual Overall	Gold
Vault	Silver
Asymmetric Bars	Bronze
Beam	Gold
Floor	Gold

1975 European Championships, Skien
Floor	Bronze

1975 World Cup, London
Individual Overall	Gold
Vault	Gold
Asymmetric Bars	Gold
Beam	Gold
Floor	Gold

1976 Olympic Games, Montreal
Team	Gold
Individual Overall	Bronze
Vault	Silver
Floor	Silver

Ludmila was one of the most respected women gymnasts of the Soviet team. She won more titles than any other gymnast. She showed her coolness under stress when the asymmetric bars collapsed as she was about to finish her routine in the World Cup in 1975.

Mitsuo Tsukahara (born 1947, Japan)
1972 Olympic Games, Munich
Team	Gold
Rings	Bronze
High Bar	Gold

1975 World Cup, London
Rings	Gold
Parallel Bars	Joint Silver
High Bar	Gold

1976 Olympic Games, Montreal
Team	Gold
Individual Overall	Bronze
Vault	Silver
Parallel Bars	Bronze
High Bar	Gold

1978 World Championships, Strasbourg
Team	Gold

Retired but far from forgotten, he is famous for having a vault exercise named after him, known as the Tsukahara. This has at least 4 variations and can be performed straight, tucked, full twisting or piked. All are high-tariff scoring vaults.

Natalia Yurchenko (born 1966, USSR)
1980 World Cup, Beijing
Individual Overall	10th

1982 World Cup, Zagreb
Individual Overall	Joint Gold
Vault	Joint Gold
Asymmetric Bars	Joint Silver
Beam	Gold
Floor	Joint 4th

1983 World Championships, Budapest
Team	Gold
Individual Overall	Gold
Vault	8th

1983 European Championships, Goteborg
Individual Overall	10th

1985 World Championships, Montreal
Team	Gold
Individual Overall	6th
Vault	6th
Beam	6th

Natalia Yurchenko invented the 'Yurchenko' vault, the most difficult vault ever invented for a woman gymnast. It would be impossible today to become a world or Olympic champion without at least one type of 'Yurchenko' vault in your repertoire.

Index

Figures in *italics* refer to illustrations

PRINTED IN BELGIUM BY
proost
INTERNATIONAL BOOK PRODUCTION

39c 6-98